NO FEAR SHA

NO FEAR SHAKESPEARE

NO FEAR SHAKESPEARE

CORIOLANUS

*sparknotes

ISBN 978-1-4549-2803-4

Distributed in Canada by Sterling Publishing Co., Inc.
c/o Canadian Manda Group, 664 Annette Street
Toronto, Ontario M6S 2C8, Canada
Distributed in the United Kingdom by GMC Distribution Services
Castle Place, 166 High Street, Lewes, East Sussex BN7 1XU, England
Distributed in Australia by NewSouth Books
45 Beach Street, Coogee, NSW 2034, Australia

For information about custom editions, special sales, and premium
and corporate purchases, please contact Sterling Special Sales at
800-805-5489 or specialsales@sterlingpublishing.com.

Manufactured in the United States of America

Lot #:
2 4 6 8 10 9 7 5 3 1

10/17

sterlingpublishing.com
sparknotes.com

Cover and title page illustration by Richard Amari.

There's matter in these sighs, these profound heaves.
You must translate: 'tis fit we understand them.

(*Hamlet,* 4.1.1–2)

FEAR NOT.

Have you ever found yourself looking at a Shakespeare play, then down at the footnotes, then back up at the play, and still not understanding? You know what the individual words mean, but they don't add up. SparkNotes' *No Fear Shakespeare* will help you break through all that. Put the pieces together with our easy-to-read translations. Soon you'll be reading Shakespeare's own words fearlessly—and actually enjoying it.

No Fear Shakespeare puts Shakespeare's language side-by-side with a facing-page translation into modern English—the kind of English people actually speak today. When Shakespeare's words make your head spin, our translation will help you sort out what's happening, who's saying what, and why.

CORIOLANUS

Characters ix

CHARACTERS

Caius Martius—A Roman general. He is given the name "Coriolanus" after he leads the Roman armies to victory against the Volscian city of Corioles. Brave, fearsome in battle, and extremely honorable, he is also overly proud, immature, inflexible, and stubbornly aristocratic. These faults, combined with a fierce contempt for the lower classes of Rome, lead to his exile from his native city.

Volumnia—A Roman noblewoman and the mother of Coriolanus. She is devoted to her son and delights in his military exploits, having raised him to be a warrior. He, in turn, often allows himself to be dominated by her iron will.

Menenius—A Roman nobleman, or patrician, and a friend to Coriolanus. Gifted with a clever tongue, he has a reputation as a great wit, which he uses adeptly to avoid conflict.

Brutus—One of the tribunes elected by the common people, or plebeians, of Rome to serve as their representative in the government. A clever politician, he regards Coriolanus as a great danger to the class he represents and to the Roman state and works to keep him out of power.

Sicinius—A Roman tribune, a clever politician, and Brutus's ally in the struggle against Coriolanus.

Tullus Aufidius—A general of the Volscians, who are Rome's enemies. He is Coriolanus's great rival in warfare but is not quite the equal of the Roman general, and his inability to defeat Coriolanus rankles him.

Cominius—A patrician of Rome and a former consul. He is a friend of Coriolanus, and he's one of the generals who leads the Roman army against the Volscians.

Titus Lartius—An old Roman nobleman. He is appointed, along with Cominius, as a general against the Volscians.

Virgilia—A Roman noblewoman and Coriolanus's loyal wife.

Valeria—A Roman noblewoman. She is close friends with Virgilia and Volumnia.

Young Martius—Coriolanus and Virgilia's son.

CORIOLANUS

ACT ONE
SCENE 1

Rome. A street.
Enter a company of mutinous CITIZENS, *with staves, clubs,*
and other weapons

FIRST CITIZEN

Before we proceed any further, hear me speak.

ALL

Speak, speak.

FIRST CITIZEN

You are all resolved rather to die than to famish?

ALL

Resolved. Resolved.

FIRST CITIZEN

5   First, you know Caius Martius is chief enemy to
the people.

ALL

We know't, we know't.

FIRST CITIZEN

Let us kill him, and we'll have corn at our own price.
Is' t a verdict?

ALL

10   No more talking on't; let it be done. Away, away!

SECOND CITIZEN

One word, good citizens.

FIRST CITIZEN

We are accounted poor citizens, the patricians good.
What authority surfeits on would relieve us. If they
would yield us but the superfluity, while it were
15   wholesome, we might guess they relieved us humanely.
But they think we are too dear: the leanness that afflicts
us, the object of our misery, is as an inventory to
particularize their abundance; our sufferance is a gain to

ACT ONE
SCENE 1

A street in Rome.
A mob of angry CITIZENS *enters. They are carrying staffs,*
clubs, and other weapons.

FIRST CITIZEN

Before we go any further, listen to me.

ALL

Speak, speak.

FIRST CITIZEN

Are you all certain that you'd rather die fighting than
starve to death?

ALL

Yes, we're certain.

FIRST CITIZEN

As you know, Caius Martius is our chief enemy.

ALL

Yes, we know that.

FIRST CITIZEN

Let's kill him, so we can sell our corn at the price we
choose. Are we agreed?

ALL

No need to talk about this anymore—let's do it. Let's go.

SECOND CITIZEN

May I speak, good citizens?

FIRST CITIZEN

We're poor. The nobles are rich. The nobles have so
much to eat that they overindulge and get sick, but if
they'd only give us their excess food, we wouldn't be
starving any longer. We'd think they were compassionate
if they helped us, but they think it's too expensive to feed
us and we don't deserve to eat. They look at our thin,
starving bodies and see them as a measure of their own

20   them. Let us revenge this with our pikes, ere we become
rakes; for the gods know I speak this in hunger for bread,
not in thirst for revenge.

SECOND CITIZEN
Would you proceed especially against Caius Martius?

ALL
Against him first. He's a very dog to the commonalty.

SECOND CITIZEN
Consider you what services he has done for his country?

FIRST CITIZEN
25   Very well, and could be content to give him good report
for 't, but that he pays himself with being proud.

SECOND CITIZEN
Nay, but speak not maliciously.

FIRST CITIZEN
I say unto you, what he hath done famously, he did it to
that end: though soft-conscienced men can be content to
30   say it was for his country he did it to please his mother
and to be partly proud; which he is, even till the altitude
of his virtue.

SECOND CITIZEN
What he cannot help in his nature, you account a vice in
him. You must in no way say he is covetous.

FIRST CITIZEN
35   If I must not, I need not be barren of accusations.
He hath faults, with surplus, to tire in repetition.

Shouts within.
What shouts are these? The other side o' the city is risen.
Why stay we prating here? To the Capitol!

ALL
Come, come.

abundance. Our suffering shows them how much they have. Let's seek revenge with our pitchforks before we become as thin as rakes. The gods know I only say this because I'm hungry for bread, not thirsty for revenge.

SECOND CITIZEN

Would you attack Caius Martius in particular?

ALL

We should attack him first. He's like a cruel dog to the people.

SECOND CITIZEN

Have you considered the ways he has served our country?

FIRST CITIZEN

I've considered them very well, and I'd be happy to honor him for his service, except he already honors himself with his pride.

SECOND CITIZEN

Don't speak so harshly.

FIRST CITIZEN

Listen, all that he's famous for doing, he did simply to become famous. Slow-witted men can be content to say he acted on behalf of his country, but the truth is that he fought to please his mother and also, in part, out of pride. He has just as much pride as courage.

SECOND CITIZEN

You call it a vice, but being proud is his nature. And you can't accuse him of being interested in the spoils of war.

FIRST CITIZEN

Even if I stop accusing him of pride, I'll still have plenty of other complaints against him. He has so many faults, I'm tired of repeating them to you.

Shouts come from offstage.

Who's shouting? The other side of the city is taking action. Why are we standing around talking? Let's go to the capitol!

ALL

Let's go.

Enter MENENIUS AGRIPPA.

FIRST CITIZEN

40   Soft! who comes here?

SECOND CITIZEN

Worthy Menenius Agrippa, one that hath always loved
the people.

FIRST CITIZEN

He's one honest enough: would all the rest were so!

MENENIUS

What work's, my countrymen, in hand? where go you

45   With bats and clubs? The matter? speak, I pray you.

SECOND CITIZEN

Our business is not unknown to th' senate; they have
had inkling this fortnight what we intend to do, which
now we'll show 'em in deeds. They say poor suitors have
strong breaths: they shall know we have strong arms too.

MENENIUS

50   Why, masters, my good friends, mine honest neighbors,
Will you undo yourselves?

SECOND CITIZEN

We cannot, sir, we are undone already.

MENENIUS

I tell you, friends, most charitable care
Have the patricians of you. For your wants,

55   Your suffering in this dearth, you may as well
Strike at the heaven with your staves as lift them
Against the Roman state, whose course will on
The way it takes, cracking ten thousand curbs
Of more strong link asunder than can ever

60   Appear in your impediment. For the dearth,
The gods, not the patricians, make it, and
Your knees to them, not arms, must help. Alack,
You are transported by calamity
Thither where more attends you, and you slander

65   The helms o' th' state, who care for you like fathers,
When you curse them as enemies.

MENENIUS AGRIPPA *enters.*

FIRST CITIZEN

Wait, who's coming?

SECOND CITIZEN

It's worthy Menenius Agrippa, who has always loved
the people.

FIRST CITIZEN

He's decent enough. I wish that all the other nobles were!

MENENIUS

What are you working on, my countrymen? Where are
you going with bats and clubs? What's the matter? Please
tell me.

SECOND CITIZEN

The Senate knows what we're upset about. They've known
for two weeks what we intend to do, and now we're going
to show them. They say poor workers have bad breath.
They're about to find out that we have strong arms too.

MENENIUS

My good friends, my honest neighbors, why will you
harm yourselves?

SECOND CITIZEN

We're already hurt.

MENENIUS

I tell you, friends, the nobles take very good care of you.
For the relief you want from your suffering, you'd do
just as well to rise up against the heavens as against the
Roman state. The Senate isn't going to change its course.
However strong a chain you form, the Senate will break
you because it's ten thousand times stronger. The gods,
not the nobles, are responsible for whatever you lack,
therefore you should fall to your knees and pray, not raise
your arms and fight. You're getting carried away by your
calamity, and you're only inviting more trouble. You're
slandering the senators, cursing them as your enemies,
without realizing that they care for you just as fathers care
for their children.

SECOND CITIZEN

Care for us! True, indeed! They ne'er cared for us
yet: suffer us to famish, and their store-houses
crammed with grain; make edicts for usury, to
support usurers; repeal daily any wholesome act
established against the rich, and provide more
piercing statutes daily, to chain up and restrain
the poor. If the wars eat us not up, they will; and
there's all the love they bear us.

MENENIUS

Either you must
Confess yourselves wondrous malicious,
Or be accused of folly. I shall tell you
A pretty tale: it may be you have heard it;
But, since it serves my purpose, I will venture
To stale 't a little more.

SECOND CITIZEN

Well, I'll hear it, sir: yet you must not think to fob off our
disgrace with a tale: but, an 't please you, deliver.

MENENIUS

There was a time when all the body's members
Rebell'd against the belly, thus accused it:
That only like a gulf it did remain
I' the midst o' the body, idle and unactive,
Still cupboarding the viand, never bearing
Like labour with the rest, where the other instruments
Did see and hear, devise, instruct, walk, feel,
And, mutually participate, did minister
Unto the appetite and affection common
Of the whole body. The belly answer'd—

SECOND CITIZEN

Well, sir, what answer made the belly?

MENENIUS

Sir, I shall tell you. With a kind of smile,
Which ne'er came from the lungs, but even thus—
For, look you, I may make the belly smile

SECOND CITIZEN

Care for us? As if! They've never cared for us. They force us to starve while their storehouses are full of grain. They make laws about loaning money that protect the loan sharks. Every day they repeal the laws that interfere with the interests of the wealthy and instead make strict laws to chain up and restrain the poor. If the wars we fight in don't kill us, these laws will. That's how well they care for us.

MENENIUS

You must either admit that you're being extremely malicious or you'll be accused of foolishness. I'll tell you a relevant story. You may have heard it, but since it illustrates my point, I'll venture to tell it again.

SECOND CITIZEN

Well, I'll listen sir, but don't think you can trick us out of our suffering with a story. But if it pleases you, tell it.

MENENIUS

There was a time when all the body's parts rebelled against the belly. They accused the belly of being an idle, inactive pool in the middle the body, always hoarding the food, never working as much as the rest of the parts. The other body parts did see and hear, think, instruct, walk, feel, and together worked for the needs and desires of the whole body. The belly answered—

SECOND CITIZEN

Well, sir, what did the belly answer?

MENENIUS

Sir, I'll tell you. With a disdainful smile—look, I can make the belly smile as well as speak—the belly tauntingly replied to the aggravated, mutinous parts that

As well as speak—it tauntingly replied
To the discontented members, the mutinous parts
That envied his receipt; even so most fitly
100   As you malign our senators for that
They are not such as you.

SECOND CITIZEN

Your belly's answer? What!
The kingly-crowned head, the vigilant eye,
The counsellor heart, the arm our soldier,
105   Our steed the leg, the tongue our trumpeter.
With other muniments and petty helps
In this our fabric, if that they—

MENENIUS

What then?
'Fore me, this fellow speaks! What then? what then?

SECOND CITIZEN

110   Should by the cormorant belly be restrain'd,
Who is the sink o' the body,—

MENENIUS

Well, what then?

SECOND CITIZEN

The former agents, if they did complain,
What could the belly answer?

MENENIUS

115   I will tell you
If you'll bestow a small—of what you have little—
Patience awhile, you'll hear the belly's answer.

SECOND CITIZEN

Ye're long about it.

MENENIUS

Note me this, good friend;
120   Your most grave belly was deliberate,
Not rash like his accusers, and thus answer'd:
"True is it, my incorporate friends," quoth he,
"That I receive the general food at first,
Which you do live upon; and fit it is,

envied the food it received—much like you who rightly accuse our senators for not starving as you do.

SECOND CITIZEN

What did the belly say? That the regal head, the watchful eye, the wise heart, the fighting arms, the mobile legs, the expressive tongue, with some small help from the other parts, if they—

MENENIUS

What then? My word, you're quite a speaker! What then? What then?

SECOND CITIZEN

The greedy belly, the sink of the body, should be restrained—

MENENIUS

And then what?

SECOND CITIZEN

If the parts complained, what could the belly answer?

MENENIUS

I'll tell you. If you'll exercise a little bit of what little patience you have, you'll hear the belly's answer.

SECOND CITIZEN

You're taking a long time to tell it.

MENENIUS

Pay attention, good friend. The belly was serious and deliberate, not rash like his accusers, and so he answered, "It's true, my fellow parts," he said, "That I am first to receive the food supply that you live on. This is as

Because I am the store-house and the shop
Of the whole body: but, if you do remember,
I send it through the rivers of your blood,
Even to the court, the heart, to the seat o' the brain;
And, through the cranks and offices of man,
130 The strongest nerves and small inferior veins
From me receive that natural competency
Whereby they live: and though that all at once,
You, my good friends,"—this says the belly, mark me—

SECOND CITIZEN
Ay, sir; well, well.

MENENIUS
135 "Though all at once cannot
See what I do deliver out to each,
Yet I can make my audit up, that all
From me do back receive the flour of all,
And leave me but the bran." What say you to't?

SECOND CITIZEN
140 It was an answer: how apply you this?

MENENIUS
The senators of Rome are this good belly,
And you the mutinous members; for examine
Their counsels and their cares, digest things rightly
Touching the weal o' the common, you shall find
145 No public benefit which you receive
But it proceeds or comes from them to you
And no way from yourselves. What do you think,
You, the great toe of this assembly?

SECOND CITIZEN
I the great toe! why the great toe?

MENENIUS
150 For that, being one o' the lowest, basest, poorest,
Of this most wise rebellion, thou go'st foremost:
Thou rascal, that art worst in blood to run,
Lead'st first to win some vantage.
But make you ready your stiff bats and clubs:

it should be, because I am the storehouse and the shop of the whole body. But if you'll remember, I send it through the rivers of your blood, even to the court of the heart, to the throne of the brain, and through the ducts and chambers of the body, the strongest nerves and the smallest veins receive from me all that they need to survive. And despite all that, you, my good friends," says the belly—

SECOND CITIZEN

Yes, sir, go on.

MENENIUS

"Even though all the parts can't see at once what I deliver to each one, I can confirm that all parts receive from me all the flour I get, and that all I'm left with is the bran." What do you say that?

SECOND CITIZEN

It's an answer. How does it apply to us?

MENENIUS

The senators of Rome are this good belly, and you are the unhappy parts. Examine their decisions and their responsibilities, see how they relate to the common good, and you'll find that there is no public benefit that you receive that doesn't come from them to you. Nothing is being taken from you. What do you think, you, the big toe of this assembly?

SECOND CITIZEN

I am the big toe? Why the big toe?

MENENIUS

For the fact that you're the leader of these ignorant rebels who are the lowest, basest, poorest of men. You're like a stray dog that runs after whatever it can catch first. But

Rome and her rats are at the point of battle;
The one side must have bale.

Enter CAIUS MARTIUS.

Hail, noble Martius!

MARTIUS
Thanks. What's the matter, you dissentious rogues,
That, rubbing the poor itch of your opinion,
160 Make yourselves scabs?

SECOND CITIZEN
We have ever your good word.

MARTIUS
He that will give good words to thee will flatter
Beneath abhorring. What would you have, you curs,
That like nor peace nor war? the one affrights you,
165 The other makes you proud. He that trusts to you,
Where he should find you lions, finds you hares;
Where foxes, geese: you are no surer, no,
Than is the coal of fire upon the ice,
Or hailstone in the sun. Your virtue is
170 To make him worthy whose offence subdues him
And curse that justice did it.
Who deserves greatness
Deserves your hate; and your affections are
A sick man's appetite, who desires most that
175 Which would increase his evil. He that depends
Upon your favours swims with fins of lead
And hews down oaks with rushes. Hang ye! Trust Ye?
With every minute you do change a mind,
And call him noble that was now your hate,
180 Him vile that was your garland. What's the matter,
That in these several places of the city
You cry against the noble senate, who,
Under the gods, keep you in awe, which else
Would feed on one another? What's their seeking?

prepare your sturdy bats and clubs: Rome and you, her rats, are at the point of battle. One side is going to lose.

CAIUS MARTIUS *enters.*

Hail, noble Martius!

MARTIUS

Thanks. What's the matter, you dissenting rebels? Are you making yourselves miserable by rubbing the minor itch of your opinion?

SECOND CITIZEN

You always speak kindly to us.

MARTIUS

Whoever speaks kindly to you flatters you undeservingly. What do you want, you dogs, who are satisfied by neither peace nor war? The one frightens you, and the other makes you self-righteous. Whoever trusts you sees you as lions, though he should see you as hares, and sees you as foxes, though he should see you as geese. You're as unstable as a burning coal on ice or a hailstone in the sun. Your nature is to honor those who should be punished for their crimes and then to curse the justice that punishes him. He who deserves greatness deserves your scorn. Your instincts are perverted: you most desire the things that will make you sicker. He who depends on your approval swims with fins of lead and cuts down oaks with blades of grass. You should be hanged! Trust you? You change your mind every minute. You call the man you hated a moment ago "noble," and you call the one you used to praise "vile." Why do you cry against the noble Senate all around the city? Second only to the gods, they take care of you, you who would otherwise eat each other alive. What do the people want?

MENENIUS

185   For corn at their own rates; whereof, they say,
       The city is well stored.

MARTIUS

                                    Hang 'em! They say?
       They'll sit by the fire, and presume to know
       What's done i' the Capitol; who's like to rise,
190   Who thrives and who declines; side factions and give out
       Conjectural marriages; making parties strong
       And feebling such as stand not in their liking
       Below their cobbled shoes. They say there's grain enough!
       Would the nobility lay aside their ruth,
195   And let me use my sword, I'll make a quarry
       With thousands of these quarter'd slaves, as high
       As I could pick my lance.

MENENIUS

       Nay, these are almost thoroughly persuaded;
       For though abundantly they lack discretion,
200   Yet are they passing cowardly. But, I beseech you,
       What says the other troop?

MARTIUS

                              They are dissolved: hang 'em!
       They said they were an-hungry; sigh'd forth proverbs,
       That hunger broke stone walls, that dogs must eat,
205   That meat was made for mouths, that the gods sent not
       Corn for the rich men only: with these shreds
       They vented their complainings; which being answer'd,
       And a petition granted them, a strange one—
       To break the heart of generosity,
210   And make bold power look pale—they threw their caps
       As they would hang them on the horns o' the moon,
       Shouting their emulation.

MENENIUS

                              What is granted them?

MENENIUS

They want to sell corn at their own rates. They say the
city has plenty.

MARTIUS

Hang them if that's what they say! They'll sit by the fire
and presume to know what goes on in the capitol: who's
likely to rise, who thrives, and who declines. They'll take
sides with factions and make hasty alliances, making
some groups strong and squashing those they don't like
beneath their cheap shoes. They say there's enough grain?
If the nobility would stop taking pity on the poor and let
me use my sword, I'd slaughter these thousands of slaves
into a pile of pieces as high as I could throw my lance.

MENENIUS

No, they've almost all calmed down. Even though they
make a scene, they're actually very cowardly. But tell me:
What happened with the other group of rebels?

MARTIUS

They've disbanded. Hang them! They said they were
hungry, they quoted proverbs: That hunger broke stone
walls, that dogs must eat, that meat was made for mouths,
that the gods didn't send corn only for the rich. With
these small statements they vented their complaints, and
when the nobles answered by granting them a petition—
which is unusual because it breaks the solidarity of the
nobles and makes them look weak—they threw their caps
into the air with joy, shouting their delight.

MENENIUS

What was granted to them?

MARTIUS

Five tribunes to defend their vulgar wisdoms,
215   Of their own choice: one's Junius Brutus,
Sicinius Velutus, and I know not—'Sdeath!
The rabble should have first unroof'd the city,
Ere so prevail'd with me: it will in time
Win upon power and throw forth greater themes
220   For insurrection's arguing.

MENENIUS

This is strange.

MARTIUS

Go, get you home, you fragments!

Enter a MESSENGER, *hastily.*

MESSENGER

Where's Caius Martius?

MARTIUS

                Here: what's the matter?

MESSENGER

225   The news is, sir, the Volsces are in arms.

MARTIUS

I am glad on 't: then we shall ha' means to vent
Our musty superfluity. See, our best elders.

Enter SICINIUS VELUTUS, JUNIUS BRUTUS, COMINIUS, TITUS
LARTIUS, *with other Senators.*

FIRST SENATOR

Martius, 'tis true that you have lately told us;
The Volsces are in arms.

MARTIUS

                 They have a leader,
230   Tullus Aufidius, that will put you to 't.
I sin in envying his nobility,

MARTIUS

> Five representatives of their own choosing to defend their ignorant views. Junius Brutus, Sicinius Velutus, and I don't know who else. God's death! The rebels would have to tear the roofs off the city before they could ever prevail upon me to grant them that. They'll soon become more powerful and make more arguments for insurrection.

MENENIUS

> This is strange.

MARTIUS

> *(to the rebels)* Go home, you crumbs!

> *A* **MESSENGER** *enters quickly.*

MESSENGER

> Where's Caius Martius?

MARTIUS

> I'm here. What's going on?

MESSENGER

> Sir, the news is that the Volsces are prepared to fight.

MARTIUS

> I'm glad about this. This means we'll have a way to get rid of our excess population. Look, here come our best elders.

> **SICINIUS VELUTUS, JUNIUS BRUTUS**, *(two Tribunes),* **COMINIUS, TITUS LARTIUS**, *and other Senators enter.*

FIRST SENATOR

> Martius, it's true what you've been telling us lately: the Volsces are ready to fight.

MARTIUS

> They have a leader, Tullus Aufidius, who will put you to the test. It's a sin, but I envy his leadership. If I could be anyone other than who I am, I would only wish to be him.

And were I any thing but what I am,
I would wish me only he.

COMINIUS

235   You have fought together?

MARTIUS

Were half to half the world by the ears and he.
Upon my party, I'ld revolt to make
Only my wars with him: he is a lion
That I am proud to hunt.

FIRST SENATOR

240   Then, worthy Martius,
Attend upon Cominius to these wars.

COMINIUS

It is your former promise.

MARTIUS

                                    Sir, it is;
And I am constant. Titus Lartius, thou
245   Shalt see me once more strike at Tullus's face.
What, art thou stiff? stand'st out?

LARTIUS

                                              No, Caius Martius;
I'll lean upon one crutch and fight with t'other,
Ere stay behind this business.

MENENIUS

250   O, true bred!

FIRST SENATOR

Your company to the Capitol; where, I know,
Our greatest friends attend us.

LARTIUS

(To COMINIUS*)*   Lead you on.
(To MARTIUS*)* Follow Cominius. We must follow you;
255   Right worthy you priority.

COMINIUS

                                         Noble Martius!

FIRST SENATOR

(To the CITIZENS*)* Hence to your homes; be gone!

COMINIUS

You've fought each other?

MARTIUS

If a quarter of the world were fighting and he were on my side, I'd revolt to fight only him. He's a lion that I am proud to hunt.

FIRST SENATOR

Then, worthy Martius, help Cominius with these wars.

COMINIUS

As you promised earlier.

MARTIUS

Sir, I did, and I'll keep my word. Titus Lartius, you'll see me strike at Tullus's face once more. Are you hesitating? Do you not want to fight?

LARTIUS

No, Caius Martius, I'll lean upon one crutch and fight with the other before I stay out of this business.

MENENIUS

Oh, you were raised to fight!

FIRST SENATOR

Let's go to the capitol. I know our greatest friends wait for us there.

LARTIUS

(to COMINIUS*)* Take the lead.

(to MARTIUS*)* Follow Cominius, and we'll follow you. You deserve to go before us.

COMINIUS

Noble Martius!

FIRST SENATOR

(to the CITIZENS*)* Go now to your homes, be gone.

MARTIUS
Nay, let them follow:
The Volsces have much corn; take these rats thither
To gnaw their garners.

CITIZENS steal away.

260   Worshipful mutiners,
Your valour puts well forth: pray, follow.

They exit. SICINIUS *and* BRUTUS *remain.*

SICINIUS
Was ever man so proud as is this Martius?
BRUTUS
He has no equal.
SICINIUS
When we were chosen tribunes for the people—
BRUTUS
265   Mark'd you his lip and eyes?
SICINIUS
                              Nay, but his taunts.
BRUTUS
Being moved, he will not spare to gird the gods—
SICINIUS
Bemock the modest moon.
BRUTUS
The present wars devour him: he is grown
270   Too proud to be so valiant.
SICINIUS
                              Such a nature,
Tickled with good success, disdains the shadow
Which he treads on at noon: but I do wonder
His insolence can brook to be commanded
275   Under Cominius.
BRUTUS
                              Fame, at the which he aims,
In whom already he's well graced, can not

MARTIUS

No, let them follow us. The Volsces have a lot of corn.
Take these rats to gnaw at their granaries.

CITIZENS sneak away.

Worshipful rebels, your courage is impressive, please
follow us.

All but SICINIUS and BRUTUS exit.

SICINIUS

Was there ever a man as proud as Martius?

BRUTUS

He has no equal.

SICINIUS

When we were chosen as representatives for the people—

BRUTUS

Did you notice his lip and eyes?

SICINIUS

No, only his taunts.

BRUTUS

When he's angry, he'll even taunt the gods.

SICINIUS

He'd mock the calmness of the moon.

BRUTUS

May this war destroy him! His courage has made him
too proud.

SICINIUS

A nature such as his, which has been amplified by all his
successes, disdains his own shadow, which he walks on
at noon. I wonder if his pride can handle being under
Cominius's command.

BRUTUS

The fame he aims for, and with which he has already
been graced, can't be maintained or increased in any

Better be held nor more attain'd than by
A place below the first: for what miscarries
280 Shall be the general's fault, though he perform
To the utmost of a man, and giddy censure
Will then cry out of Martius "O if he
Had borne the business!"

SICINIUS

                                        Besides, if things go well,
285 Opinion that so sticks on Martius shall
Of his demerits rob Cominius.

BRUTUS

                                        Come:
Half all Cominius' honours are to Martius.
Though Martius earned them not, and all his faults
290 To Martius shall be honous, though indeed
In aught he merit not.

SICINIUS

                                Let's hence, and hear
How the dispatch is made, and in what fashion,
More than his singularity, he goes
295 Upon this present action.

BRUTUS

                                Let's along.

                                                        They exit.

position other than the lead. Whatever goes wrong will be seen as the general's fault, even though he'll do the best job a man could do, and fickle public opinion will then say of Martius, "Oh, if only he had been in charge!"

SICINIUS

Besides, if things go well, public opinion that favors Martius will steal praise away from Cominius.

BRUTUS

Indeed, half of all Cominius's victories have been credited to Martius, though he didn't win them. And whatever faults Cominius has are seen as Martius's honors, though Martius really doesn't have any merit.

SICINIUS

Let's go and hear what's happening. Let's see how, our feelings about his personality aside, he prepares for this battle.

BRUTUS

Let's go.

They exit.

ACT 1, SCENE 2

Corioles. The Senate House.
Enter TULLUS AUFIDIUS *and certain Senators.*

FIRST SENATOR

So, your opinion is, Aufidius,
That they of Rome are entered in our counsels
And know how we proceed.

AUFIDIUS

Is it not yours?
What ever have been thought on in this state,
That could be brought to bodily act ere Rome
Had circumvention? 'Tis not four days gone
Since I heard thence; these are the words: I think
I have the letter here; yes, here it is.

He reads.

"They have press'd a power, but it is not known
Whether for east or west: the dearth is great;
The people mutinous; and it is rumour'd,
Cominius, Martius your old enemy,
Who is of Rome worse hated than of you,
And Titus Lartius, a most valiant Roman,
These three lead on this preparation
Whither 'tis bent: most likely 'tis for you:
Consider of it."

FIRST SENATOR

Our army's in the field
We never yet made doubt but Rome was ready
To answer us.

AUFIDIUS

Nor did you think it folly
To keep your great pretences veil'd till when
They needs must show themselves; which in
      the hatching,
It seem'd, appear'd to Rome. By the discovery.
We shall be shorten'd in our aim, which was

ACT 1, SCENE 2

The Senate house in Corioles.
TULLUS AUFIDIUS *and Senators of Corioles enter.*

FIRST SENATOR

So Aufidius, your opinion is that the Romans have spied on our council and know how we proceed.

AUFIDIUS

Don't you agree? Haven't all the plans we've ever discussed here that could be put into action against Rome been thwarted? Not even four days have gone by since I heard from the field, these are the words—I think I have the letter here—yes, here it is.

He reads.

"They've raised an army, but it's not known whether they will march east or west. The famine is serious, the people are rebelling, and it's rumored that Cominius, your old enemy Martius—whom the Romans hate worse than you—and Titus Lartius, a most valiant Roman, these three lead the attack, wherever it's headed. Most likely toward you. Think about it."

FIRST SENATOR

Our army's in the field. We've never doubted that the Romans were ready to fight back.

AUFIDIUS

You thought it was wise to keep your plans secret until they needed to be revealed, but it seems that the Romans knew your plans as soon as they were hatched. Since they know our intention, we can't proceed as we had planned:

To take in many towns ere almost Rome
Should know we were afoot.

SECOND SENATOR

Noble Aufidius,
Take your commission; hie you to your bands:
30 Let us alone to guard Corioles:
If they set down before 's, for the remove
Bring your army; but, I think, you'll find
They've not prepared for us.

AUFIDIUS

O, doubt not that;
35 I speak from certainties. Nay, more,
Some parcels of their power are forth already,
And only hitherward. I leave your honours.
If we and Caius Martius chance to meet,
'Tis sworn between us we shall ever strike
40 Till one can do no more.

ALL

The gods assist you!

AUFIDIUS

And keep your honours safe!

FIRST SENATOR

Farewell.

SECOND SENATOR

Farewell.

ALL

45 Farewell.

Exeunt.

to capture as many towns as possible before the Romans
knew we were moving toward them.

SECOND SENATOR

Noble Aufidius, do your duty. Go to your men. Leave us
here to guard Corioles ourselves. If they attack us, bring
your army back before they take the city, but I think
you'll find they haven't prepared for us.

AUFIDIUS

Don't be so sure. I'm certain when I say that some part of
their army is already moving toward us. I leave you now,
noblemen. If we happen to meet Caius Martius, he and I
have sworn that we'll always strike at each other until one
of us can strike no more.

ALL

May the gods be with you!

AUFIDIUS

And keep you noblemen safe!

FIRST SENATOR

Farewell.

SECOND SENATOR

Farewell.

ALL

Farewell.

They exit.

ACT 1, SCENE 3

Rome. A room in Martius's house.
Enter VOLUMNIA *and* VIRGILIA, *mother and wife to* MARTIUS.
They set them down on two low stools, and sew.

VOLUMNIA

I pray you, daughter, sing; or express yourself in a more
comfortable sort: if my son were my husband, I should
freelier rejoice in that absence wherein he won honour
than in the embracements of his bed where he would
5   show most love. When yet he was but tender-bodied and
the only son of my womb, when youth with comeliness
plucked all gaze his way, when for a day of kings'
entreaties a mother should not sell him an hour from her
beholding, I, considering how honour would become
10   such a person—that it was no better than picture-like to
hang by the wall, if renown made it not stir—was pleased
to let him seek danger where he was like to find fame.
To a cruel war I sent him; from whence he returned, his
brows bound with oak. I tell thee, daughter, I sprang not
15   more in joy at first hearing he was a man-child than now
in first seeing he had proved himself a man.

VIRGILIA

But had he died in the business, madam; how then?

VOLUMNIA

Then his good report should have been my son; I therein
would have found issue. Hear me profess sincerely: had
20   I a dozen sons, each in my love alike and none less dear
than thine and my good Martius, I had rather had eleven
die nobly for their country than one voluptuously surfeit
out of action.

Enter a GENTLEWOMAN.

ACT 1, SCENE 3

A room in Martius's house in Rome.
VOLUMNIA *and* VIRGILIA, *mother and wife of Martius, enter.*
They sit down on two low stools and sew.

VOLUMNIA

Please, my daughter-in-law, sing or express yourself
more cheerfully. If my son were my husband, I would
be happier with him away winning honors than lovingly
embracing me in bed. Before he was full grown, when he
was still my only child, when he was boyishly handsome
and attracting much attention, when even if the king
begged me I shouldn't have let him out of my sight for an
hour, I considered how honored he would become, and
that unless he were inspired to make a name for himself,
he would be no better than a picture hanging on the wall,
so I happily let him face danger, because that's how he
was likely to find fame. I sent him to a cruel war from
which he returned crowned with garlands of oak. I tell
you, daughter-in-law, I jumped for joy more to see that
he had proven himself as a man than I did when I first
heard he was a boy child.

VIRGILIA

But if had he died in the war, madam? How would you
have felt then?

VOLUMNIA

Then his noble deeds would have been my son—in them
I would have found my legacy. Listen to me seriously: if
I had a dozen sons and loved them equally, as much as I
love our Martius, I would rather that eleven of them die
nobly for their country than one choose the pleasures of
making love over doing his duty.

A GENTLEWOMAN *enters.*

GENTLEWOMAN
    Madam, the Lady Valeria is come to visit you.

VIRGILIA
25   (*to* VOLUMNIA) Beseech you, give me leave to retire myself.

VOLUMNIA
    Indeed, you shall not.
    Methinks I hear hither your husband's drum,
    See him pluck Aufidius down by the hair,
    As children from a bear, the Volsces shunning him:
30   Methinks I see him stamp thus, and call thus:
    "Come on, you cowards! you were got in fear,
    Though you were born in Rome:" His bloody brow
    With his mail'd hand then wiping, forth he goes,
    Like to a harvest-man that's task'd to mow
35   Or all or lose his hire.

VIRGILIA
    His bloody brow! O Jupiter, no blood!

VOLUMNIA
    Away, you fool! it more becomes a man
    Than gilt his trophy: the breasts of Hecuba,
    When she did suckle Hector, look'd not lovelier
40   Than Hector's forehead when it spit forth blood
    At Grecian sword, contemning. Tell Valeria,
    We are fit to bid her welcome.

                            Exit GENTLEWOMAN.

VIRGILIA
    Heavens bless my lord from fell Aufidius!

VOLUMNIA
    He'll beat Aufidius's head below his knee
45   And tread upon his neck.

    Enter VALERIA, *with an usher and a gentlewoman.*

GENTLEWOMAN

(to VOLUMNIA*)* Madam, the Lady Valeria has come to see you.

VIRGILIA

May I please be excused to have some time alone?

VOLUMNIA

No, you may not. I think I hear your husband's drum coming toward us. He must have plucked out all Aufidius's hairs so the Volsces will avoid him the way children run from a bear. I think I see him stamping like this, and calling like this: "Come on, you cowards! You were born in fear even though you were born in Rome." He's wiping his bloody forehead with his armored hand. He's unrelenting like a laborer who must harvest a whole field or not be paid at all.

VIRGILIA

His bloody forehead! O, Jupiter, king of the gods, not blood!

VOLUMNIA

Don't be foolish! Blood belongs on a man more than gold belongs on his trophy. When Hecuba suckled Hector, her breasts were no lovelier than Hector's forehead when a Grecian sword struck it and it gushed furiously with blood. Tell Valeria that we welcome her in.

The GENTLEWOMAN *exits.*

VIRGILIA

Heavens protect my husband from the deadly Aufidius!

VOLUMNIA

He'll beat Aufidius's head down below his knees and then stand on his neck.

VALERIA *enters with an usher and a gentlewoman.*

VALERIA

My ladies both, good day to you.

VOLUMNIA

Sweet madam.

VIRGILIA

I am glad to see your ladyship.

VALERIA

How do you both? you are manifest house-keepers. What
50   are you sewing here? A fine spot, in good faith. How does
your little son?

VIRGILIA

I thank your ladyship; well, good madam.

VOLUMNIA

He had rather see the swords, and hear a drum, than
look upon his school-master.

VALERIA

55   O' my word, the father's son: I'll swear, 'tis a very pretty
boy. O' my troth, I looked upon him o' Wednesday half
an hour together: H'as such a confirmed countenance. I
saw him run after a gilded butterfly: and when he caught
it, he let it go again; and after it again; and over and over
60   he comes, and again; catched it again; or whether his fall
enraged him, or how 'twas, he did so set his teeth and tear
it; O, I warrant it, how he mammocked it!

VOLUMNIA

One on 's father's moods.

VALERIA

Indeed, la, 'tis a noble child.

VIRGILIA

65   A crack, madam.

VALERIA

Come, lay aside your stitchery; I must have you play the
idle housewife with me this afternoon.

VIRGILIA

No, good madam; I will not out of doors.

VALERIA

My ladies, good day to you both.

VOLUMNIA

Sweet madam.

VIRGILIA

I'm glad to see you, your ladyship.

VALERIA

How are you both? You are remarkable house-keepers. *(to Volumnia)* What are you sewing here? It looks like fine embroidery. *(to Virgilia)* How is your little son?

VIRGILIA

Thank you, your ladyship. He's fine, good madam.

VOLUMNIA

He'd rather see the soldiers and hear a drum than do his schoolwork.

VALERIA

It's true, he's his father's son. He's a very good-looking boy. I spent half an hour with him on Wednesday. He is so determined. I saw him run after a golden butterfly, and when he caught it, he let it go and then went after it again. He fell down and got back up and again he caught the butterfly. I don't know whether his fall enraged him or what, but he clenched his teeth and tore it. I tell you, he ripped it apart!

VOLUMNIA

He has his father's moods.

VALERIA

Indeed, dear, he's a noble child.

VIRGILIA

He's devilish, madam.

VALERIA

Set aside your stitching. Pretend to be an idle housewife with me this afternoon.

VIRGILIA

No, good madam. I can't go out today.

VALERIA

Not out of doors!

VOLUMNIA

70   She shall, she shall.

VIRGILIA

Indeed, no, by your patience; I'll not over the threshold
till my lord return from the wars.

VALERIA

Fie, you confine yourself most unreasonably: come, you
must go visit the good lady that lies in.

VIRGILIA

75   I will wish her speedy strength, and visit her with my
prayers; but I cannot go thither.

VOLUMNIA

Why, I pray you?

VIRGILIA

'Tis not to save labour, nor that I want love.

VALERIA

You would be another Penelope: yet, they say, all the
80   yarn she spun in Ulysses' absence did but fill Ithaca full
of moths. Come; I would your cambric were sensible
as your finger, that you might leave pricking it for pity.
Come, you shall go with us.

VIRGILIA

No, good madam, pardon me; indeed, I will not forth.

VALERIA

85   In truth, la, go with me; and I'll tell you excellent news of
your husband.

VIRGILIA

O, good madam, there can be none yet.

VALERIA

Verily, I do not jest with you; there came news from him
last night.

VIRGILIA

90   Indeed, madam!

VALERIA

Can't go out?

VOLUMNIA

She will, she will.

VIRGILIA

No. Please let me stay in. I won't cross the threshold until my husband returns from the war.

VALERIA

You're being unreasonable to confine yourself. Come, you must go visit our neighbor, who's expecting a baby.

VIRGILIA

I wish her an easy birth and send her my prayers, but I can't go see her.

VOLUMNIA

Why not?

VIRGILIA

It's not because I'm lazy or don't care for her.

VALERIA

You're like another Penelope, except they say that all the yarn she spun in Ulysses's absence only filled Ithaca with moths. I wish your embroidery cloth were as sensitive as your finger, that way you might take pity on it and stop pricking it. Come with us.

VIRGILIA

No, good madam, please excuse me. I won't go.

VALERIA

Truly, come with me, and I'll tell you excellent news about your husband.

VIRGILIA

Oh, good madam, there can't be good news yet.

VALERIA

I'm not kidding you. News came from him last night.

VIRGILIA

Really, madam?

VALERIA

> In earnest, it's true; I heard a senator speak it. Thus it is:
> the Volsces have an army forth; against
> whom Cominius the general is gone, with one part of our
> Roman power: your lord and Titus Lartius are set down
95   before their city Corioles; they nothing doubt prevailing
> and to make it brief wars. This is true, on mine honour;
> and so, I pray, go with us.

VIRGILIA

> Give me excuse, good madam; I will obey you in every
> thing hereafter.

VOLUMNIA

100   (*to Valeria*) Let her alone, lady: as she is now, she will but
> disease our better mirth.

VALERIA

> In troth, I think she would. Fare you well, then. Come,
> good sweet lady. Prithee, Virgilia, turn thy solemness out
> o' door and go along with us.

VIRGILIA

105   No, at a word, madam; indeed, I must not. I wish you
> much mirth.

VALERIA

> Well, then, farewell.

Exeunt.

VALERIA

Yes, it's true. I heard a senator talking. He said Cominius
the general is leading one part of our Roman army against
the oncoming Volsces. Your husband and Titus Lartius
are attacking their city, Corioles. They have no doubt
that they'll win and that the battle won't last long. On my
honor, this news is true. Please come out with us.

VIRGILIA

Forgive me, good madam. I'll do as you say from now on.

VOLUMNIA

(to Valeria) Let her stay home, lady. The way she is now,
she'll only detract from our celebration.

VALERIA

I think you're right—she will. Cheer up then, good sweet
lady. Please, Virgilia, shake off your sad mood and come
out with us.

VIRGILIA

No. In a word, madam, I simply can't. I wish you much
happiness.

VALERIA

Well then, goodbye.

They all exit.

ACT 1, SCENE 4

Before Corioles.
Enter, with drum and colours, MARTIUS, TITUS LARTIUS,
Captains and Soldiers. To them a MESSENGER

MARTIUS
Yonder comes news. A wager they have met.

LARTIUS
My horse to yours, no.

MARTIUS
                                        'Tis done.

LARTIUS
                                                    Agreed.

MARTIUS
5   (*to* MESSENGER) Say, has our general met the enemy?

MESSENGER
They lie in view; but have not spoke as yet.

LARTIUS
So, the good horse is mine.

MARTIUS
                                        I'll buy him of you.

LARTIUS
No, I'll nor sell nor give him: lend you him I will
10   For half a hundred years. Summon the town.

MARTIUS
How far off lie these armies?

MESSENGER
Within this mile and half.

MARTIUS
Then shall we hear their 'larum, and they ours.
Now, Mars, I prithee, make us quick in work,
15   That we with smoking swords may march from hence,
To help our fielded friends!

ACT 1, SCENE 4

Outside the gates of Corioles.
MARTIUS, **TITUS LARTIUS**, *captains and soldiers enter, with a drummer and trumpeter. A* **MESSENGER** *comes toward them.*

MARTIUS
Here comes news. I bet there's been a battle.

LARTIUS
I bet you my horse for yours that there hasn't been a battle.

MARTIUS
It's a bet.

LARTIUS
Agreed.

MARTIUS
(*to* **MESSENGER**) Tell us, has our general been in battle with the enemy?

MESSENGER
They can see each other, but they haven't fought yet.

LARTIUS
So, your good horse is mine.

MARTIUS
I'll buy him back from you.

LARTIUS
No, I'll won't sell or give him away. I'll lend him to you for fifty years. Alert the town.

MARTIUS
How far away are the armies?

MESSENGER
Within a mile and a half.

MARTIUS
Then we'll hear their call to arms, and they'll hear ours. Now, Mars, god of war, I pray to you, make our attack quick, so that with victorious swords we may march from here to help our friends on the battlefield!

(to the trumpeter) Come, blow thy blast.

They sound a parley. Enter two SENATORS *with others on the walls.*

(to the SENATORS*)* Tullus Aufidius, is he within your walls?
FIRST SENATOR
No, nor a man that fears you less than he,
20   That's lesser than a little.

Drums afar off

(to the Volsces)   Hark! our drums
Are bringing forth our youth. We'll break our walls,
Rather than they shall pound us up: our gates,
Which yet seem shut, we, have but pinn'd with rushes;
25   They'll open of themselves.

Alarum afar off

(to the Romans)   Hark you, far off!
There is Aufidius; list, what work he makes
Amongst your cloven army.

They exit from the walls.

MARTIUS

O, they are at it!

LARTIUS
30   Their noise be our instruction. Ladders, ho!

Enter the army of the Volsces.

MARTIUS
They fear us not, but issue forth their city.
Now put your shields before your hearts, and fight
With hearts more proof than shields. Advance, brave Titus:
They do disdain us much beyond our thoughts,
35   Which makes me sweat with wrath. Come on, my fellows:
He that retires I'll take him for a Volsce,
And he shall feel mine edge.

(to the trumpeter) Come, blow your horn.

The trumpet sounds. Two Volscian SENATORS *enter, with others, on the walls of Corioles.*

(to the SENATORS) Is Tullus Aufidius inside these walls?

FIRST SENATOR

No. And there isn't a man here who fears you any less than he does, which is virtually not at all.

Drums are heard from far away.

(to the Volsces) Listen! Our drums are summoning our young soldiers. We'd rather break down our own walls than let them fence us in. Our gates, which look locked, are actually just gently shut. They'll open on their own.

A trumpet is heard from far away.

(to the Romans) Listen! In the distance, that's Aufidius. Listen to how he's beating your divided army.

They exit from the walls.

MARTIUS

Oh, they're fighting each other!

LARTIUS

Their noise tells us what to do. Raise the ladders!

The Volscian army enters.

MARTIUS

They're not afraid of us—instead they march out of their own city. Cover your hearts with your shields now and fight with hearts that are stronger than these shields. Go forward, brave Titus. They hate us more than we think, which makes me sweat with anger. Come on, my fellow soldiers. Whoever hangs back, I'll think you're a Volsce, and you'll feel the edge of my sword.

*Alarum. The Romans are beat back to their trenches. They
exit, with the Volsces following. Re-enter* MARTIUS *cursing,
with Roman soldiers.*

MARTIUS
All the contagion of the south light on you,
You shames of Rome! you herd of—Boils and plagues
40   Plaster you o'er, that you may be abhorr'd
Farther than seen and one infect another
Against the wind a mile! You souls of geese,
That bear the shapes of men, how have you run
From slaves that apes would beat! Pluto and hell!
45   All hurt behind; backs red, and faces pale
With flight and agued fear! Mend and charge home,
Or, by the fires of heaven, I'll leave the foe
And make my wars on you: look to't: come on;
If you'll stand fast, we'll beat them to their wives,
50   As they us to our trenches. Follow's!

*Another alarum. The Volsces reenter and are driven back to the
gates of Corioles, which open to admit them.*

So, now the gates are ope: now prove good seconds:
'Tis for the followers fortune widens them,
Not for the fliers: mark me, and do the like.
                              MARTIUS *follows the fleeing Volsces
                              through the gates, and is shut in.*

FIRST SOLDIER
Fool-hardiness; not I.
SECOND SOLDIER
55   Nor I.
FIRST SOLDIER
See, they have shut him in.
                              Alarum continues.

Trumpets sound. The Romans all exit, as they are beaten back to their trenches. MARTIUS *re-enters, cursing, with Roman soldiers.*

MARTIUS

I curse you with the plague of the south, you shameful Romans! You bunch of—may blisters and infection cover over you so that people will smell you before they see you, and may your disease spread on the wind for a mile, even when the wind blows against you! You look like men, but you have the souls of geese. Why did you run from slaves that even apes could beat? Pluto, god of the dead and the underworld! You ran away and didn't fight back; your backs are red with blood and your faces pale with fear! Pull yourselves together and charge again, or, by the fires of heaven, I'll stop fighting the Volsces and attack you instead. Listen, if you can hold steady, we'll beat them and take their wives. They're in our trenches. Follow me!

Another trumpet sounds. The Volsces re-enter to attack, and are driven back to the gates of Corioles, which open to admit them.

So, the gates are open now. Support me well. Fortune opens the gates for those who follow me, not for those who run from battle. Listen to me, and do as I say.

> MARTIUS *follows the fleeing Volsces*
> *through the gates, and is shut in.*

FIRST SOLDIER

That's crazy. I'm not going.

SECOND SOLDIER

Neither am I.

FIRST SOLDIER

Look, they've locked him in.

> *The trumpet continues.*

ALL
> To the pot, I warrant him.

Enter TITUS LARTIUS

LARTIUS
> What is become of Martius?

ALL
>   Slain, sir, doubtless.

FIRST SOLDIER
60   Following the fliers at the very heels,
> With them he enters; who, upon the sudden,
> Clapp'd to their gates: he is himself alone,
> To answer all the city.

LARTIUS
>   O noble fellow!
65   Who sensibly outdares his senseless sword,
> And, when it bows, stands up. Thou art left, Martius:
> A carbuncle entire, as big as thou art,
> Were not so rich a jewel. Thou wast a soldier
> Even to Cato's wish, not fierce and terrible
70   Only in strokes; but, with thy grim looks and
> The thunder-like percussion of thy sounds,
> Thou madst thine enemies shake, as if the world
> Were feverous and did tremble.

Enter MARTIUS, *bleeding, assaulted by the enemy.*

FIRST SOLDIER
> Look, sir.

LARTIUS
75   O,'tis Martius!
> Let's fetch him off, or make remain alike.
>   *They fight, and all enter the city, exiting the stage.*

ALL

> I'm sure he'll end up in their cooking pot.

TITUS LARTIUS *re-enters.*

LARTIUS

> What happened to Martius?

ALL

> He has undoubtedly been killed, sir.

FIRST SOLDIER

> He followed right behind the fleeing Volsces and entered
> the city with them. They closed the gates behind him,
> and he's in there all alone to fight the whole city.

LARTIUS

> Oh, noble fellow! He's braver than his sword, which
> cannot feel pain, and he stands firm while even his
> sword bends. You are done for, Martius. A flawless
> red gem, as large as you, wouldn't be as valuable a
> jewel as you are. You were the soldier **Cato** would
> have wished for, not just fierce and terrible on
> occasion, but with your serious looks and your
> thunderous voice, you terrified your enemies as if the
> whole world were shaking with a fever.

*A military adviser
in ancient Rome.*

MARTIUS *re-enters, bleeding, having been assaulted by the
Volsces.*

FIRST SOLDIER

> Look, sir.

LARTIUS

> Oh, it's Martius! Let's rescue him or we'll be assaulted by
> the Volsces, too.
>> *They fight, and all enter the city, exiting the stage.*

ACT 1, SCENE 5

Corioles. A street.
Enter certain ROMANS, *with spoils*

FIRST ROMAN
    This will I carry to Rome.

SECOND ROMAN
    And I this.

THIRD ROMAN
    A murrain on't! I took this for silver.

Enter MARTIUS *and* TITUS LARTIUS *with a trumpet.*

MARTIUS
    See here these movers that do prize their hours
5   At a crack'd drachma. Cushions, leaden spoons,
    Irons of a doit, doublets that hangmen would
    Bury with those that wore them, these base slaves,
    Ere yet the fight be done, pack up: down with them!
                  The ROMANS *with spoils exit.*
                 Alarum continues still afar off

    And hark, what noise the general makes! To him!
10   There is the man of my soul's hate, Aufidius,
    Piercing our Romans: then, valiant Titus, take
    Convenient numbers to make good the city;
    Whilst I, with those that have the spirit, will haste
    To help Cominius.

LARTIUS
15   Worthy sir, thou bleed'st;
    Thy exercise hath been too violent for
    A second course of fight.

ACT 1, SCENE 5

A street in Corioles.
Some ROMANS *enter with spoils of war.*

FIRST ROMAN

I'll bring this back to Rome.

SECOND ROMAN

And I'll bring this.

THIRD ROMAN

Curse it! I thought this was silver.

MARTIUS *(bleeding) and* TITUS LARTIUS *enter with a*
trumpeter.

MARTIUS

Look at these scavengers who spend their time gathering
worthless coins! Cushions, lead spoons, cheap swords,
clothes that hangmen would bury along with whoever
died wearing them. These lowly slaves are packing up
before the fight is even over. They're the worst!

> *(The* ROMANS *with spoils leave.*
> *Trumpets still continue far away.)*

And listen to the noise Cominius makes! Let's go help
him! Aufidius, the one my soul hates, is driving our
Roman army apart. Valiant Titus, take enough men with
you to secure the city. I'll go now with those who have the
spirit and help Cominius.

LARTIUS

Worthy sir, you're bleeding. Your efforts have been too
violent for you to fight again now.

MARTIUS

        Sir, praise me not;
My work hath yet not warm'd me: fare you well:
20   The blood I drop is rather physical
Than dangerous to me: to Aufidius thus
I will appear, and fight.

LARTIUS

Now the fair goddess, Fortune,
Fall deep in love with thee; and her great charms
25   Misguide thy opposers' swords! Bold gentleman,
Prosperity be thy page!

MARTIUS

        Thy friend no less
Than those she placeth highest! So, farewell.

LARTIUS

Thou worthiest Martius!

Exit **MARTIUS**.

30   Go, sound thy trumpet in the market-place;
Call thither all the officers o' the town,
Where they shall know our mind: away!

Exeunt.

MARTIUS

Don't flatter me. I'm not even warmed up yet. Good luck to you. Bleeding is more helpful to me than it is dangerous. I'll find Aufidius and fight.

LARTIUS

May the fair goddess Fortune fall deeply in love with you, and may she cast a spell on your opponents so their swords don't strike you! Brave gentlemen, may you be successful!

MARTIUS

May Fortune be no less a friend to you than she is to those she loves most! Good luck.

LARTIUS

You're the bravest, Martius!

MARTIUS exits.

Go, sound your trumpet in the marketplace. Bring all the town officials here. We'll tell them what we're thinking. Go!

All exit, going in different directions.

ACT 1, SCENE 6

Near the camp of Cominius.
Enter COMINIUS, *as it were in retire, with soldiers.*

COMINIUS

Breathe you, my friends: well fought; we are come off
Like Romans, neither foolish in our stands,
Nor cowardly in retire: believe me, sirs,
We shall be charged again. Whiles we have struck,
5   By interims and conveying gusts we have heard
The charges of our friends. The Roman gods!
Lead their successes as we wish our own,
That both our powers, with smiling fronts encountering,
May give you thankful sacrifice.

Enter a MESSENGER.

10   Thy news?
MESSENGER

The citizens of Corioles have issued,
And given to Lartius and to Martius battle:
I saw our party to their trenches driven,
And then I came away.
COMINIUS

15   Though thou speak'st truth,
Methinks thou speak'st not well. How long is 't since?
MESSENGER

Above an hour, my lord.
COMINIUS

'Tis not a mile; briefly we heard their drums:
How couldst thou in a mile confound an hour,
20   And bring thy news so late?

ACT 1, SCENE 6

Near Cominius's camp.
COMINIUS *enters with soldiers, appearing to retreat from battle.*

COMINIUS
Catch your breath, my friends. You fought well. We've
cleared the enemy like Romans, neither foolish in our
attacks nor cowardly in our retreat. Believe me, sirs,
we'll fight again. While we've been attacking, news has
intermittently come to us, carried on the winds, about
the battles fought by our friends. O, Roman gods! Grant
them the success that we wish for as well, and may both
our armies, with smiling faces, then gratefully offer you
a sacrifice.

A MESSENGER *enters.*

What news do you have?

MESSENGER
The citizens of Corioles have left the city and are fighting
with Lartius and Martius. Our group was driven to their
trenches, and then I got away.

COMINIUS
You're telling the truth, but you're leaving something
out. How long ago did this happen?

MESSENGER
More than an hour ago, my lord.

COMINIUS
They're not even a mile away. A little while ago we heard
their drums. How could you waste an hour traveling only
one mile and bring your news so late?

MESSENGER
                                        Spies of the Volsces
Held me in chase, that I was forced to wheel
Three or four miles about, else had I, sir,
Half an hour since brought my report.

He exits.

COMINIUS
25   Who's yonder,
That does appear as he were flay'd? O gods
He has the stamp of Martius; and I have
Before-time seen him thus.

MARTIUS
   (*from offstage*)   Come I too late?

COMINIUS
30   The shepherd knows not thunder from a tabour
More than I know the sound of Martius' tongue
From every meaner man.

Enter MARTIUS.

MARTIUS
                                        Come I too late?

COMINIUS
Ay, if you come not in the blood of others,
35   But mantled in your own.

MARTIUS
                                        O, let me clip ye
In arms as sound as when I woo'd, in heart
As merry as when our nuptial day was done,
And tapers burn'd to bedward!

They embrace.

COMINIUS
40   Flower of warriors, how is it with Titus Lartius?

MESSENGER

Volscian spies chased me and I was forced to go three or four miles out of my way. Otherwise I would have brought my report half an hour earlier.

He exits.

COMINIUS

Who's over there, looking like he's been skinned alive? Oh, gods, it looks like Martius, and I've seen him look like this before.

MARTIUS

(from offstage) Am I too late?

COMINIUS

I know the difference between the sound of Martius's tongue and every lesser man even more than the shepherd knows the difference between the sound of thunder and a drum.

MARTIUS *enters, covered in blood.*

MARTIUS

Am I too late?

COMINIUS

Yes, but only if you're drenched in your own blood, not the blood of others.

MARTIUS

Oh, let me hug you with arms as strong as when I wooed my wife, with a heart as happy as the day we married and the candles burned down, telling us it was time for bed!

They embrace.

COMINIUS

Prized warrior, how is Titus Lartius?

MARTIUS

As with a man busied about decrees:
Condemning some to death, and some to exile;
Ransoming him, or pitying, threatening the other;
Holding Corioles in the name of Rome,
45   Even like a fawning greyhound in the leash,
To let him slip at will.

COMINIUS

                                    Where is that slave
Which told me they had beat you to your trenches?
Where is he? call him hither.

MARTIUS

50   Let him alone;
He did inform the truth: but for our gentlemen,
The common file—a plague! tribunes for them!—
The mouse ne'er shunn'd the cat as they did budge
From rascals worse than they.

COMINIUS

55   But how prevail'd you?

MARTIUS

Will the time serve to tell? I do not think.
Where is the enemy? are you lords o' the field?
If not, why cease you till you are so?

COMINIUS

Martius, we have at disadvantage fought and did
60   Retire to win our purpose.

MARTIUS

How lies their battle? know you on which side
They have placed their men of trust?

COMINIUS

                                    As I guess, Martius,
Their bands i' the vaward are the Antiates,
65   Of their best trust; o'er them Aufidius,
Their very heart of hope.

MARTIUS

He's busy with decrees: condemning some to death and some to exile, releasing men for ransom or pity, and threatening others. He's holding Corioles in the name of Rome, as if the city were a greyhound on a leash, eager to please and ready to run.

COMINIUS

Where is that slave who told me they had beaten you back to your trenches? Where is he? Call him here.

MARTIUS

Leave him alone. He told the truth. But as for our men, the common soldiers, I curse them with a plague! May they be tried in court! Like stray dogs, they ran away from the Volsces, who are lower-bred than they are. They ran like a mouse runs from a cat.

COMINIUS

How did you triumph then?

MARTIUS

Do I have enough time to tell you? I don't think so. Where is the enemy? Have you captured this field? If not, why did you stop before you did?

COMINIUS

Martius, we've been fighting without enough soldiers or supplies, so we retreated temporarily to regroup, and then we'll win.

MARTIUS

What's their battle formation? Do you know what side their best men are on?

COMINIUS

My guess, Martius, is that the Antiates, whom they trust highly, are in the front. Leading them is Aufidius, the very heart of their hope.

MARTIUS

                              I do beseech you,
By all the battles wherein we have fought,
By the blood we have shed together, by the vows
70   We have made to endure friends, that you directly
Set me against Aufidius and his Antiates;
And that you not delay the present, but,
Filling the air with swords advanced and darts,
We prove this very hour.

COMINIUS

75   Though I could wish
You were conducted to a gentle bath
And balms applied to, you, yet dare I never
Deny your asking: take your choice of those
That best can aid your action.

MARTIUS

80   Those are they
That most are willing. If any such be here—
As it were sin to doubt—that love this painting
Wherein you see me smear'd; if any fear
Lesser his person than an ill report;
85   If any think brave death outweighs bad life
And that his country's dearer than himself;
Let him alone, or so many so minded,
Wave thus, to express his disposition,
And follow Martius.

                              He waves his sword.
             They all shout and wave their swords, take him
                      up in their arms, and cast up their caps.

90   O, me alone! make you a sword of me?
If these shows be not outward, which of you
But is four Volsces? none of you but is
Able to bear against the great Aufidius
A shield as hard as his. A certain number,
95   Though thanks to all, must I select from all: the rest
Shall bear the business in some other fight,

MARTIUS

By all the battles we've fought, by the blood we have shed together and by the vows we made to remain friends, I beg that you put me directly against Aufidius and his Antiates. And that you not hesitate but rather fill the air with raised swords and darts. Now is the time for us to prove ourselves.

COMINIUS

I wish you were going now to a gentle bath and to have balms applied to you, but I never dare to deny what you ask. Take your choice of the men who can best help you.

MARTIUS

The men I choose are the ones most eager to fight. If there is any man here—and it would be a sin to doubt it— who loves seeing me smeared in blood, that fears more for his honor than for his personal safety, that thinks a brave death outweighs a bad life, and that his country is more important than himself, let him alone, or others if they feel the same, wave their arms now to tell me who they are. And then follow me.

He waves his sword.
They all shout and wave their swords, lift him up
in their arms, and throw their caps in the air.

Choose me! Make me one of your swordsmen! If these aren't just superficial words, are there four among you who aren't traitors? All of you would be able to fight the great Aufidius—your shields are as hard as his. I will only select four men, but thank you, all of you. The rest of you will fight our enemy in some other battle when the time comes. Please march, and I'll quickly choose which men are best suited to this fight.

As cause will be obey'd. Please you to march;
And I shall quickly draw out my command,
Which men are best inclined.

COMINIUS

100   March on, my fellows:
Make good this ostentation, and you shall
Divide in all with us.

Exeunt.

COMINIUS

> March forward, men. Perform well, and we'll all share the honor.

All exit.

ACT 1, SCENE 7

The gates of Corioles.
TITUS LARTIUS, having set a guard upon Corioles, going with
drum and trumpet toward COMINIUS and CAIUS MARTIUS,
enters with LIEUTENANT, other Soldiers, and a Scout.

LARTIUS
So, let the ports be guarded: keep your duties,
As I have set them down. If I do send, dispatch
Those centuries to our aid: the rest will serve
For a short holding: if we lose the field,
5   We cannot keep the town.

LIEUTENANT
                                    Fear not our care, sir.

LARTIUS
Hence, and shut your gates upon's.
(*to the scout*) Our guider, come; to the Roman camp
        conduct us.

                                                    Exeunt.

ACT 1, SCENE 7

The gates of Corioles.

TITUS LARTIUS, *leaving someone to guard Corioles, goes toward* COMINIUS *and* CAIUS MARTIUS *with a drummer and trumpeter. A* LIEUTENANT, *other soldiers, and a scout also enter.*

LARTIUS

Guard the gate. Do your job as I've explained it. If I send a message, send those hundreds of soldiers to help us. The remaining soldiers can hold the city on their own for a little while. After all, if we lose in the field, we can't keep the city anyway.

LIEUTENANT

Don't worry, sir, we'll guard the city.

LARTIUS

Good, and shut these gates once I'm gone. Here comes our scout to bring us to the Roman camp.

They exit.

ACT 1, SCENE 8

A field of battle.
Alarum as in battle. Enter, from opposite sides, **MARTIUS** *and*
AUFIDIUS.

MARTIUS
>   I'll fight with none but thee; for I do hate thee
>   Worse than a promise-breaker.

AUFIDIUS
>   We hate alike:
>   Not Afric owns a serpent I abhor
> 5 More than thy fame and envy. Fix thy foot.

MARTIUS
>   Let the first budger die the other's slave,
>   And the gods doom him after!

AUFIDIUS
>   If I fly, Martius,
>   Holloa me like a hare.

MARTIUS
> 10   Within these three hours, Tullus,
>   Alone I fought in your Corioles walls,
>   And made what work I pleased: 'tis not my blood
>   Wherein thou seest me mask'd; for thy revenge
>   Wrench up thy power to the highest.

AUFIDIUS
> 15   Wert thou the Hector
>   That was the whip of your bragg'd progeny,
>   Thou shouldst not scape me here.
>   *They fight, and certain Volsces come to the aid of* **AUFIDIUS**.
>   Officious, and not valiant, you have shamed me
>   In your condemned seconds.
>   **MARTIUS** *fights till they be driven in breathless.*
>   **AUFIDIUS** *and* **MARTIUS** *exit separately.*
>   *Exeunt.*

ACT 1, SCENE 8

A battlefield.
A trumpet sounds from the battle. MARTIUS *and* AUFIDIUS
enter from opposite sides.

MARTIUS

> I'll fight only against you, because I hate you worse than
> a traitor.

AUFIDIUS

> We feel the same hatred. There's not a snake in Africa
> that I hate more than your fame and envy. Prepare
> to fight.

MARTIUS

> Whoever runs away from this fight first must become
> the other's slave until death, and after that may the gods
> curse him!

AUFIDIUS

> If I run, Martius, hunt me like a hare.

MARTIUS

> Less than three hours ago, Tullus, I fought alone inside
> the walls of Corioles, and I killed whoever I wanted.
> It's not my own blood you see me covered in. For your
> revenge, fight me with your fullest force.

AUFIDIUS

> If you're anything like Hector, the failed champion of
> your ancestors whom you're so proud of, you won't
> escape me here.
>
> > *They fight, and some Volsces come to the aid of* AUFIDIUS.
> You're arrogant, not brave. You've shamed me with your
> assistance, and I condemn you for it.
>
> > > MARTIUS *fights until they're out of breath.*
>
> > > > *All exit.*

ACT 1, SCENE 9

The Roman camp.
Alarum. A retreat is sounded. Flourish. Enter, from one side,
COMINIUS *with the Romans; from the other side,* MARTIUS,
with his arm in a scarf.

COMINIUS
    (*to* MARTIUS) If I should tell thee o'er this thy day's work,
    Thou'ldst not believe thy deeds: but I'll report it
    Where senators shall mingle tears with smiles,
    Where great patricians shall attend and shrug,
5   I' the end admire, where ladies shall be frighted,
    And, gladly quaked, hear more; where the dull tribunes,
    That, with the fusty plebeians, hate thine honours,
    Shall say against their hearts "We thank the gods
    Our Rome hath such a soldier."
10   Yet camest thou to a morsel of this feast,
    Having fully dined before.

Enter TITUS LARTIUS, *with his power, from the pursuit.*

LARTIUS
                    O general,
    Here is the steed, we the caparison:
    Hadst thou beheld—
MARTIUS
15   Pray now, no more: my mother,
    Who has a charter to extol her blood,
    When she does praise me grieves me. I have done
    As you have done; that's what I can; induced
    As you have been; that's for my country:
20   He that has but effected his good will
    Hath overta'en mine act.
COMINIUS
                You shall not be
    The grave of your deserving; Rome must know

ACT 1, SCENE 9

The Roman camp.
Trumpets blast to announce Roman victory. A retreat signal is
also sounded. COMINIUS *and the Romans enter from one side.*
MARTIUS, *with his arm in a sling, enters from the other side.*

COMINIUS

> If I told you about all you did today, you wouldn't believe
> it. But when I tell the senators, they'll both cry and smile.
> Great noblemen will pause, shrug their shoulders in
> bewilderment, and wonder. Ladies will be frightened,
> happily frightened, and ask to hear more. The somber
> tribunes, who along with the moldy peasants hate it when
> you triumph, will say under their breath: "We thank the
> gods that Rome has a soldier like you." But for you this
> victory was only like a small bite, since you had already
> had a feast of victory before.

> TITUS LARTIUS, *with his army, enters, returning from the*
> *pursuit.*

LARTIUS

> Oh, general, Martius was like the horse, and we were
> only along for the ride. If you had seen—

MARTIUS

> Please, say no more. My mother, who has a right to praise
> me since I am her son, irritates me when she does so. I've
> done what you've done: I've done the best I can. I was
> trained as you were: to serve my country. Whoever has
> done what he intended to do has accomplished more than
> I have.

COMINIUS

> Don't dismiss the praise you deserve. Rome must know
> your value as her soldier. To conceal your achievements

The value of her own: 'twere a concealment
25 Worse than a theft, no less than a traducement,
To hide your doings; and to silence that,
Which, to the spire and top of praises vouch'd,
Would seem but modest: therefore, I beseech you—
In sign of what you are, not to reward
30 What you have done—before our army hear me.

MARTIUS

I have some wounds upon me, and they smart
To hear themselves remember'd.

COMINIUS

                                            Should they not,
Well might they fester 'gainst ingratitude,
35 And tent themselves with death. Of all the horses,
Whereof we have ta'en good and good store, of all
The treasure in this field achieved and city,
We render you the tenth, to be ta'en forth,
Before the common distribution, at
40 Your only choice.

MARTIUS

                                    I thank you, general;
But cannot make my heart consent to take
A bribe to pay my sword: I do refuse it;
And stand upon my common part with those
45 That have beheld the doing.

A long flourish. They all cry "Martius! Martius!" and cast up
their caps and lances: COMINIUS *and* LARTIUS *stand bare.*

MARTIUS

May these same instruments, which you profane,
Never sound more! when drums and trumpets shall
I' the field prove flatterers, let courts and cities be
Made all of false-faced soothing!
50 When steel grows soft as the parasite's silk,
Let him be made an orator for the wars!
No more, I say! For that I have not wash'd
My nose that bled, or foil'd some debile wretch.—

would be worse than stealing, and not less than slander, because for what you have done, no matter how highly we praise you, it will never be sufficient. So I ask you—in recognition of your importance to Rome, not to boast of your achievements—let me address you in front of our army.

MARTIUS

I'm wounded, and my wounds hurt when they hear how I got them.

COMINIUS

If your wounds don't hear, they might think we're ungrateful, become infected, and cause your death. Of all the many good horses we've taken from the enemy and of all the treasures we've won on the battlefield and in the city, we'll give you one-tenth to take now, before the rest is divided among us. Take whatever you choose.

MARTIUS

Thank you, general, but my heart won't take a bribe to pay my sword. I refuse to stand there and listen to my deeds be told to those who saw me do them.

A long trumpet blast is heard. They all cry "Martius! Martius!" and throw their caps and lances into the air.
COMINIUS *and* LARTIUS *stand respectfully without their hats*

MARTIUS

May these instruments, which you play in the wrong moment, never make a sound again! If drums and trumpets could flatter the enemy into submission in battle, then we should build our courts and cities on their false praise! When steel grows soft as the diplomat's silk, let us make an army of diplomats! Stop all this flattery! Because I haven't washed my bloody nose or because I triumphed over some weakling—which, you fail to note,

Which, without note, here's many else have done,—
55   You shout me forth
In acclamations hyperbolical;
As if I loved my little should be dieted
In praises sauced with lies.

COMINIUS
                              Too modest are you;
60   More cruel to your good report than grateful
To us that give you truly: by your patience,
If 'gainst yourself you be incensed, we'll put you,
Like one that means his proper harm, in manacles,
Then reason safely with you. Therefore, be it known,
65   As to us, to all the world, that Caius Martius
Wears this war's garland: in token of the which,
My noble steed, known to the camp, I give him,
With all his trim belonging; and from this time,
For what he did before Corioles, call him,
70   With all the applause and clamour of the host,
Martius Caius Coriolanus! Bear
The addition nobly ever!
                    Flourish. Trumpets sound, and drums.

ALL
Martius Caius Coriolanus!

CORIOLANUS
                              I will go wash;
75   And when my face is fair, you shall perceive
Whether I blush or no: howbeit, I thank you.
I mean to stride your steed, and at all times
To undercrest your good addition
To the fairness of my power.

COMINIUS
                              So, to our tent;
80   Where, ere we do repose us, we will write
To Rome of our success. You, Titus Lartius,
Must to Corioles back: send us to Rome
The best, with whom we may articulate,
85   For their own good and ours.

many others have done, too—you praise me in overstated terms, as if I enjoyed having my small achievements puffed up with exaggerations.

COMINIUS

You're too modest. You express more resentment about the praise we offer than you express gratitude for our true account of your service. Allow me to suggest that if you're going to get upset, we'll tie you up as we would someone suicidal and then reason with you. It must be known, not only to us but to all the world, that Caius Martius is the hero of this war. So I give you my magnificent horse, whose value is known to our men, and all his equipment. And from this time on, in honor of what you did in Corioles, you will be called, with all the applause and clamor you deserve, Caius Martius Coriolanus! Use this additional title nobly, always!

Trumpets sound and drums pound.

ALL

Caius Martius Coriolanus!

CORIOLANUS

I'll go wash and when my face is clean, you'll see whether or not I'm blushing. Thank you for this honor. I'll ride your horse and try always to live up to this noble title you have given me.

COMINIUS

Let's go to our tent. Before we rest, we'll write to Rome of our success. You, Titus Lartius, must go back to Corioles. Send us the best citizen of Corioles with whom we may negotiate a treaty, one that is fair to them and to us.

LARTIUS

I shall, my lord.

CORIOLANUS

The gods begin to mock me. I, that now
Refused most princely gifts, am bound to beg
Of my lord general.

COMINIUS

90   Take't; 'tis yours. What is 't?

CORIOLANUS

I sometime lay here in Corioles
At a poor man's house; he used me kindly:
He cried to me; I saw him prisoner;
But then Aufidius was with in my view,
95   And wrath o'erwhelm'd my pity: I request you
To give my poor host freedom.

COMINIUS

O, well begg'd!
Were he the butcher of my son, he should
Be free as is the wind. Deliver him, Titus.

LARTIUS

100   Martius, his name?

CORIOLANUS

By Jupiter, forgot!
I am weary; yea, my memory is tired.
Have we no wine here?

COMINIUS

Go we to our tent:
105   The blood upon your visage dries; 'tis time
It should be look'd to: come.

Exeunt.

LARTIUS

> I will, my lord.

CORIOLANUS

> The gods begin to mock me. I, who just refused amazing
> gifts, must now beg something of you, my lord general.

COMINIUS

> Whatever you want is yours. What is it?

CORIOLANUS

> When I was in Corioles, I stayed for some time in a
> poor man's house. He treated me kindly, and now he's a
> prisoner. He cried out for my help, but I was focused on
> Aufidius, and anger overwhelmed my pity. I request that
> you free my poor host.

COMINIUS

> You're certainly persuasive! Even if he were the butcher
> of my son, he'd be as free as the wind. Release him, Titus.

LARTIUS

> Martius, his name?

CORIOLANUS

> By Jupiter! I've forgotten. I'm worn out and my memory
> is tired. Do we have any wine here?

COMINIUS

> Let's go our tent. The blood on your face is drying. It's
> time you were looked at. Come.

All exit.

ACT 1, SCENE 10

The camp of the Volsces.
A flourish. Cornets. Enter TULLUS AUFIDIUS, *bloody, with two*
or three soldiers.

AUFIDIUS
> The town is ta'en!

FIRST SOLDIER
> 'Twill be deliver'd back on good condition.

AUFIDIUS
> Condition!
> I would I were a Roman; for I cannot,
5   Being a Volsce, be that I am. Condition!
> What good condition can a treaty find
> I' the part that is at mercy? Five times, Martius,
> I have fought with thee: so often hast thou beat me,
> And wouldst do so, I think, should we encounter
10 As often as we eat. By the elements,
> If e'er again I meet him beard to beard,
> He's mine, or I am his: mine emulation
> Hath not that honour in't it had; for where
> I thought to crush him in an equal force,
15 True sword to sword, I'll potch at him some way
> Or wrath or craft may get him.

FIRST SOLDIER
>   He's the devil.

AUFIDIUS
> Bolder, though not so subtle. My valour's poison'd
> With only suffering stain by him; for him
20 Shall fly out of itself: nor sleep nor sanctuary,
> Being naked, sick, nor fane nor Capitol,
> The prayers of priests nor times of sacrifice,
> Embarquements all of fury, shall lift up
> Their rotten privilege and custom 'gainst
25 My hate to Martius: where I find him, were it

ACT 1, SCENE 10

The Volscian camp.
Trumpets sound. TULLUS AUFIDIUS *enters, bloody, with two or three Volscian Soldiers.*

AUFIDIUS

The town is taken!

FIRST SOLDIER

It'll be given back with fair conditions.

AUFIDIUS

Conditions! I wish I were a Roman, but I can't be other than what I am: a Volsce. Conditions! Under what conditions can a treaty be fair to the side that has lost? I've fought Martius five times, and every time he has beaten me. And I think he would beat me again in the future if we met in battle as often as we eat. By the elements, if I ever see him face to face again, I'll kill him or he'll kill me. My desire to beat him isn't as honorable as it once was, for while I once wanted to crush him with our forces being equal, fighting fairly sword to sword, now I'll stab him however I can and let either my anger or my trickery bring him down.

FIRST SOLDIER

He's the devil.

AUFIDIUS

Bolder, but not as subtle. He's the only one who has compromised my honor, and for that I will seek vengeance. Neither sleep nor sanctuary, nor being unarmed, nor sick, nor the constraints of the temple or the capitol, the prayers of priests or times of sacrifice, none of these obstacles to my fury will stop me from hating Martius. Wherever I find him, even at home in my brother's protection, despite the law of hospitality,

At home, upon my brother's guard, even there,
Against the hospitable canon, would I
Wash my fierce hand in's heart. Go you to the city;
Learn how 'tis held; and what they are that must
30   Be hostages for Rome.

FIRST SOLDIER

Will not you go?

AUFIDIUS

I am attended at the cypress grove: I pray you—
'Tis south the city mills—bring me word thither
How the world goes, that to the pace of it
35   I may spur on my journey.

FIRST SOLDIER

I shall, sir.

Exeunt.

I'll wash my fierce hand in his heart. Go to Corioles, find out how it's being occupied and who's been taken hostage by the Romans.

FIRST SOLDIER

You're not going?

AUFIDIUS

They're waiting for me at the cypress grove, south of the city mills. Please bring word to me there about how things are going so I can plan my journey accordingly.

FIRST SOLDIER

I will, sir.

All exit.

ACT TWO
SCENE 1

Rome. A public place.
Enter MENENIUS *with the two Tribunes of the people,* SICINIUS
and BRUTUS.

MENENIUS
> The augurer tells me we shall have news to-night.

BRUTUS
> Good or bad?

MENENIUS
> Not according to the prayer of the people, for they love
> not Martius.

SICINIUS
> Nature teaches beasts to know their friends.

MENENIUS
> Pray you, who does the wolf love?

SICINIUS
> The lamb.

MENENIUS
> Ay, to devour him; as the hungry plebeians would the
> noble Martius.

BRUTUS
> He's a lamb indeed, that baas like a bear.

MENENIUS
> He's a bear indeed, that lives like a lamb. You two are old
> men: tell me one thing that I shall ask you.

BOTH
> Well, sir.

MENENIUS
> In what enormity is Martius poor in, that you two have
> not in abundance?

BRUTUS
> He's poor in no one fault, but stored with all.

ACT TWO

SCENE 1

A public place in Rome.

MENENIUS *enters with* SICINIUS *and* BRUTUS, *the two tribunes of the people.*

MENENIUS

The fortuneteller tells me we'll receive news tonight.

BRUTUS

Good news or bad?

MENENIUS

Not the news people prayed for—they have no love
for Martius.

SICINIUS

In nature, animals learn who their friends are.

MENENIUS

Tell me, who does the wolf love?

SICINIUS

The lamb.

MENENIUS

Yes, to devour him, as the hungry citizens would love to
devour the noble Martius.

BRUTUS

Martius is like a lamb, a lamb that roars like a bear.

MENENIUS

Martius is like a bear, a bear that lives like a lamb. You two
have been around a long time, answer one question for me.

BOTH

What do you want to know, sir?

MENENIUS

Tell me a quality that Martius lacks but that you two
have in abundance.

BRUTUS

He doesn't have just one fault—he has every fault.

SICINIUS

Especially in pride.

BRUTUS

And topping all others in boasting.

MENENIUS

This is strange now: do you two know how you are
censured here in the city, I mean of us o' the right-hand
5   file, do you?

BOTH

Why, how are we censured?

MENENIUS

Because you talk of pride now, will you not be angry?

BOTH

Well, well, sir, well?

MENENIUS

Why, 'tis no great matter; for a very little thief of
occasion will rob you of a great deal of patience: give your
10   dispositions the reins, and be angry at your pleasures; at
the least if you take it as a pleasure to you in being so. You
blame Martius for being proud.

BRUTUS

We do it not alone, sir.

MENENIUS

I know you can do very little alone; for your helps are
15   many, or else your actions would grow wondrous single:
your abilities are too infant-like for doing much alone.
You talk of pride: O that you could turn your eyes toward
the napes of your necks, and make but an interior survey
of your good selves! O that you could!

BRUTUS

20   What then, sir?

MENENIUS

Why, then you should discover a brace of unmeriting,
proud, violent, testy magistrates, alias fools, as any
in Rome.

SICINIUS

Especially pride.

BRUTUS

And boasting, above all.

MENENIUS

One thing is strange though. Do you two know how you are regarded by the nobles of the city? Do you?

BOTH

How are we seen?

MENENIUS

Because you talk of pride now, won't you get angry if I tell you?

BOTH

No, not at all, sir.

MENENIUS

Well, it doesn't take much. Even the slightest incident will cause you to lose your patience and let your disposition take over. You become angry at what you should have enjoyed, and your only enjoyment comes from being angry. And yet you blame Martius for being proud.

BRUTUS

We're not alone in our opinion, sir.

MENENIUS

I know you can do very little alone. Without all the help you get, your actions would be totally insignificant. Your abilities aren't strong enough for you to do much on your own. You talk of pride. If only you could see yourselves as you really are! I wish you could!

BRUTUS

And what if we could, sir?

MENENIUS

You'd see that you are equal to all the other unqualified, proud, violent, testy government officials—in other words, fools—in Rome.

SICINIUS

Menenius, you are known well enough, too.

MENENIUS

25   I am known to be a humorous patrician, and one that
loves a cup of hot wine with not a drop of allaying Tiber
in't; said to be something imperfect in favouring the
first complaint; hasty and tinder-like upon too trivial
motion; one that converses more with the buttock of
30   the night than with the forehead of the morning: what I
think I utter, and spend my malice in my breath. Meeting
two such wealsmen as you are—I cannot call you
Lycurguses—if the drink you give me touch my palate
adversely, I make a crooked face at it. I can't say your
35   worships have delivered the matter well, when I find the
ass in compound with the major part of your syllables:
and though I must be content to bear with those that say
you are reverend grave men, yet they lie deadly that tell
you you have good faces. If you see this in the map of my
40   microcosm, follows it that I am known well enough too?
what harm can your bisson conspectuities glean out of
this character, if I be known well enough too?

BRUTUS

Come, sir, come, we know you well enough.

MENENIUS

You know neither me, yourselves nor any thing. You are
45   ambitious for poor knaves' caps and legs: you wear out
a good wholesome forenoon in hearing a cause between
an orange-wife and a faucet-seller; and then rejourn the
controversy of three pence to a second day of audience.
When you are hearing a matter between party and party,
50   if you chance to be pinched with the colic, you make faces
like mummers; set up the bloody flag against all patience;
and, in roaring for a chamber pot, dismiss the controversy
bleeding the more entangled by your hearing: all the
peace you make in their cause is, calling both the parties
55   knaves. You are a pair of strange ones.

SICINIUS

Menenius, you have a bad reputation, too.

MENENIUS

I'm known as a moody aristocrat, and one that loves a cup
of hot wine not diluted by even a drop of water from the
Tiber River. I'm said to be somewhat flawed as a judge
because I'm hastily swayed by the first argument I hear.
I'm quick to anger at the slightest disturbance. I stay up
late at night and don't rise early in the morning. I say
whatever I think and express my anger when I speak.
Meeting two statesmen such as yourselves—I cannot call
you lawmakers—if I don't like the drink you give me, I
make a crooked face at it. I don't think you deserve the
respectful titles of your profession, when I find most of
what you say to be asinine. And though I can tolerate
those who say you are respectable, serious men, the
ones who say you are honest are deadly liars. If you see
these same qualities in me, doesn't it make sense that
I'm known for my bad qualities? What harm can your
misperceptions do to my character, if I already have a
bad reputation?

BRUTUS

That's enough, sir. We know your reputation well.

MENENIUS

You don't know anything about me, or about yourselves.
Your ambition is to have poor citizens take off their hats
and bow down to you. You'll waste a whole morning
listening to a dispute over three pence between an orange
vendor and a wine tap seller and then postpone settling
the issue until the next day. When you're hearing a
matter between two parties, if you're feeling the tiniest
bit sick, you become very dramatic: you violently refuse
to be patient and, demanding a chamber pot, dismiss the
controversy, leaving it even more entangled as a result of
your hearing it. The only justice you show is in calling
both parties scoundrels. You're a pair of strange men.

BRUTUS

Come, come, you are well understood to be a perfecter
giber for the table than a necessary bencher in
the Capitol.

MENENIUS

Our very priests must become mockers, if they shall
60 encounter such ridiculous subjects as you are. When you
speak best unto the purpose, it is not worth the wagging of
your beards; and your beards deserve not so honourable
a grave as to stuff a botcher's cushion, or to be entombed
in an ass's pack-saddle. Yet you must be saying, Martius
65 is proud; who in a cheap estimation, is worth predecessors
since Deucalion, though peradventure some of the best of
'em were hereditary hangmen. God e'en to your worships:
more of your conversation would infect my brain, being
the herdsmen of the beastly plebeians: I will be bold to take
70 my leave of you.

BRUTUS *and* SICINIUS *stand aside.*
Enter VOLUMNIA, VIRGILIA, *and* VALERIA.

How now, my as fair as noble ladies,—and the moon,
were she earthly, no nobler,—whither do you follow your
eyes so fast?

VOLUMNIA

Honourable Menenius, my boy Martius approaches; for
75 the love of Juno, let's go.

MENENIUS

Ha? Martius coming home?

VOLUMNIA

Ay, worthy Menenius; and with most prosperous
approbation.

MENENIUS

Take my cap, Jupiter, and I thank thee. *(he throws his cap
in the air.)* Hoo! Martius coming home!

VOLUMNIA AND VIRGILIA

Nay, 'tis true.

BRUTUS

Come, come. You're well known to be a better dinner-table conversationalist than a serious judge.

MENENIUS

Even our priests would become mockers if they encountered anyone as ridiculous as you. When you stay on topic, what you say isn't worth the wagging of your beards. And your beards don't even deserve the honorable burial of being stuffed in a seamstress's cushion or being entombed in the pack saddle of a donkey. You say Martius is proud, but even guessing conservatively, he's worth all your predecessors since Deucalion, who survived the flood, even though some of them may have been hangmen. Good evening to you both. To keep talking with you would infect my brain, since you are the herdsmen of the beastly common people. I must go.

BRUTUS and SICINIUS stand aside.
VOLUMNIA, VIRGILIA, and VALERIA enter.

How are you, my dear noble ladies? You are like the moon on earth—what are you looking at?

VOLUMNIA

Honorable Menenius, my son Martius approaches. For the love of Juno, let's go.

MENENIUS

What? Martius is coming home?

VOLUMNIA

Yes, worthy Menenius, and he's proudly victorious.

MENENIUS

I take my hat off in thanks to you, Jupiter, king of the gods. *(He throws his cap in the air.)* Whew! Martius is coming home!

VOLUMNIA AND VIRGILIA

Yes, it's true.

VOLUMNIA

80   Look, here's a letter from him. *(She produces a paper.)* The
        state hath another, his wife another; and, I think, there's
        one at home for you.

MENENIUS

        I will make my very house reel tonight: a letter for me?

VIRGILIA

        Yes, certain, there's a letter for you; I saw't.

MENENIUS

85   A letter for me? It gives me an estate of seven years'
        health; in which time I will make a lip at the physician:
        the most sovereign prescription in Galen is but
        empiricutic, and, to this preservative, of no better report
        than a horse drench. Is he not wounded? He was wont to
90   come home wounded.

VIRGILIA

        O, no, no, no!

VOLUMNIA

        O, he is wounded; I thank the gods for't.

MENENIUS

        So do I too, if it be not too much: brings he victory in his
        pocket, the wounds become him.

VOLUMNIA

95   On's brows: Menenius, he comes the third time home
        with the oaken garland.

MENENIUS

        Has he disciplined Aufidius soundly?

VOLUMNIA

        Titus Lartius writes, they fought together, but
        Aufidius got off.

MENENIUS

100   And 'twas time for him too, I'll warrant him that: an he
        had stayed by him, I would not have been so 'fidiused for
        all the chests in Corioles, and the gold that's in them. Is
        the senate possessed of this?

VOLUMNIA

Look, here's a letter from him. *(She produces a paper.)* He sent another to the Senate and another to his wife. I think there's one at home for you.

MENENIUS

My household will be thrilled tonight. A letter for me!

VIRGILIA

Yes, I'm certain there's a letter for you. I saw it.

MENENIUS

A letter for me! It makes me live seven years longer, and all the while I'll laugh at my doctor. The most well-established prescription according to the great doctor Galen is nothing but an experimental cure, and compared to this news, it's worth no more than horse medicine. Is he wounded? He was likely to come home wounded.

VIRGILIA

Oh, no, no, no.

VOLUMNIA

Oh, yes, he's wounded, and I thank the gods for it.

MENENIUS

As do I, if he's not wounded too much. If he brings home victory, the wounds are badges of honor.

VOLUMNIA

He's wounded on his forehead. Menenius, this is the third time he's come home with the garland of oak.

MENENIUS

Has he thoroughly beaten Aufidius?

VOLUMNIA

Titus Lartius writes that they fought each other, but Aufidius got away.

MENENIUS

It was Aufidius's time to die. For all the chests in Corioles and the gold that's in them, I'll bet that if Martius had captured him, he would've gotten the beating he deserved. Does the Senate know about this?

VOLUMNIA

Good ladies, let's go. Yes, yes, yes; the senate has letters
105   from the general, wherein he gives my son the whole
name of the war: he hath in this action outdone his former
deeds doubly.

VALERIA

In troth, there's wondrous things spoke of him.

MENENIUS

Wondrous? Ay, I warrant you, and not without his
110   true purchasing.

VIRGILIA

The gods grant them true!

VOLUMNIA

True! pow, waw.

MENENIUS

True! I'll be sworn they are true. Where is he wounded?
(*to the tribunes*) God save your good worships! Martius
115   is coming home: he has more cause to be proud. (*to*
VOLUMNIA) Where is he wounded?

VOLUMNIA

I' the shoulder and i' the left arm there will be large
cicatrices to show the people, when he shall stand for his
place. He received in the repulse of Tarquin seven hurts i'
120   the body.

MENENIUS

One i' the neck, and two i' the thigh,—there's nine that
I know.

VOLUMNIA

He had, before this last expedition, twenty-five wounds
upon him.

MENENIUS

125   Now it's twenty-seven: every gash was an enemy's grave.
                                   A shout and flourish.

Hark! the trumpets.

VOLUMNIA

Good ladies, let's go. Yes, yes, yes! Cominius has written to the Senate and named my son responsible for the victory. His accomplishments in this war are double all his past deeds.

VALERIA

It's true, there are wonderful things said about him.

MENENIUS

Wonderful! Yes, it's true, and none that he didn't earn.

VIRGILIA

Oh, gods, may these words be true!

VOLUMNIA

True! Absolutely!

MENENIUS

True? I promise they're true. Where is he wounded? *(to the tribunes)* May you be well, good sirs! Martius is coming home. He has new reasons to be proud. *(to* **VOLUMNIA***)* Where is he wounded?

VOLUMNIA

In the shoulder and in the left arm. There will be large scars to show the people, when he stands to receive his place as consul. When he defeated the king Tarquin, he was wounded seven times.

MENENIUS

Once in the neck and twice in the thigh. There are nine wounds that I know of.

VOLUMNIA

Before this last expedition, he had twenty-five wounds in total.

MENENIUS

Now it's twenty-seven. Every gash represents an enemy who has died.

> *Trumpets sound, and a shout comes from offstage.*

Hark! The trumpets.

VOLUMNIA
These are the ushers of Martius: before him he
carries noise, and behind him he leaves tears:
130 Death, that dark spirit, in 's nervy arm doth lie;
Which, being advanced, declines, and then men die.

Trumpets sound. Enter COMINIUS *the general, and* TITUS
LARTIUS; *between them,* CORIOLANUS, *crowned with an oaken
garland; with Captains and Soldiers, and a* HERALD.

HERALD
Know, Rome, that all alone Martius did fight
Within Corioles gates: where he hath won,
With fame, a name to Martius Caius; these
135 In honour follows "Coriolanus."
Welcome to Rome, renowned Coriolanus!

Flourish.

ALL
Welcome to Rome, renowned Coriolanus!

CORIOLANUS
No more of this; it does offend my heart:
Pray now, no more.

COMINIUS
140   Look, sir, your mother!

CORIOLANUS
                                                          O,
You have, I know, petition'd all the gods
For my prosperity.

He kneels.

VOLUMNIA
                                    Nay, my good soldier, up
145 My gentle Martius, worthy Caius, and
By deed-achieving honour newly named,—
What is it?—Coriolanus must I call thee?—

Coriolanus rises.

But, O, thy wife!

VOLUMNIA

These men walk ahead of Martius to introduce him.
Many cheers welcome him, and he leaves behind many
tears. Death, that dark spirit, lies within his strong arm.
When he raises his arm, it comes down upon his enemies
and they die.

Trumpets sound in a different melody. COMINIUS, *the general,
and* TITUS LARTIUS *enter. Between them stands* CORIOLANUS
*crowned with a garland of oak, with captains and soldiers and
a* HERALD.

HERALD

Romans, let it be known that Martius fought all alone
within Corioles's gates. There he won, along with honor,
a new name. The name "Coriolanus" now respectfully
follows "Martius Caius." Welcome to Rome, the
renowned Coriolanus!

Trumpets sound.

ALL

Welcome to Rome, renowned Coriolanus!

CORIOLANUS

No more praise. I don't like it. Please now, no more.

COMINIUS

Look, sir, your mother!

CORIOLANUS

You have, I know, begged all the gods to grant me victory!

He kneels.

VOLUMNIA

No, my good soldier, get up. My gentle Martius, worthy
Caius, and through your honor achieved by your actions,
newly named—what is it?—Coriolanus must I call thee?

Coriolanus rises.

But O, your wife!

CORIOLANUS
                    My gracious silence, hail!
150   Wouldst thou have laugh'd had I come coffin'd home,
       That weep'st to see me triumph? Ah, my dear,
       Such eyes the widows in Corioles wear,
       And mothers that lack sons.

MENENIUS
                                   Now, the gods crown thee!

CORIOLANUS
155   And live you yet? *(to* VALERIA*)* O my sweet lady, pardon.

VOLUMNIA
       I know not where to turn: O, welcome home:
       And welcome, general: and you're welcome all.

MENENIUS
       A hundred thousand welcomes. I could weep
       And I could laugh, I am light and heavy. Welcome.
160   A curse begin at very root on's heart,
       That is not glad to see thee! You are three
       That Rome should dote on: yet, by the faith of men,
       We have some old crab-trees here at home that will not
       Be grafted to your relish. Yet welcome, warriors!
165   We call a nettle but a nettle and
       The faults of fools but folly.

COMINIUS
       Ever right.

CORIOLANUS
       Menenius ever, ever.

HERALD
       Give way there, and go on!

CORIOLANUS
170   *(to* VOLUMNIA *and* VIRGILIA*)* Your hand, and yours:
       Ere in our own house I do shade my head,
       The good patricians must be visited;
       From whom I have received not only greetings,
       But with them change of honours.

CORIOLANUS

There you are, my lovely silent wife! Would you have laughed if I had come home in a coffin, since you are crying to see me come home in victory? Ah, my dear, your eyes look like tose of the widows and the mothers who have lost sons in Corioles.

MENENIUS

Now, the gods crown you!

CORIOLANUS

Are you still alive? *(to* VALERIA*)* I'm sorry, my sweet lady.

VOLUMNIA

I don't know where to turn. O, welcome home! And welcome, general! Welcome all!

MENENIUS

A hundred thousand welcomes. I could weep and I could laugh. I'm happy and sad. Welcome. May a curse reach to the very root of anyone's heart who isn't happy to see you! Rome should honor you as it would three men. However, we have some bitter old men here who refuse to applaud you. But welcome, warriors! Some things just are what they are, and fools don't understand.

COMINIUS

You're right.

CORIOLANUS

You're always right, Menenius.

HERALD

Make way. Keep walking.

CORIOLANUS

(to VOLUMNIA *and* VIRGILIA*)* Give me your hands. Before I can go home and rest, I must visit the nobles because they haven't only welcomed me back but have also honored me with this new name.

VOLUMNIA

175   I have lived
        To see inherited my very wishes
        And the buildings of my fancy: only
        There's one thing wanting, which I doubt not but
        Our Rome will cast upon thee.

CORIOLANUS

180   Know, good mother,
        I had rather be their servant in my way,
        Than sway with them in theirs.

COMINIUS

                                                On, to the Capitol!
                    Flourish. Cornets. Exeunt in state, as before.
                        BRUTUS *and* **SICINIUS** *come forward.*

BRUTUS

        All tongues speak of him, and the bleared sights
185   Are spectacled to see him: your prattling nurse
        Into a rapture lets her baby cry
        While she chats him: the kitchen malkin pins
        Her richest lockram 'bout her reechy neck,
        Clambering the walls to eye him: stalls, bulks, windows,
190   Are smother'd up, leads fill'd, and ridges horsed
        With variable complexions, all agreeing
        In earnestness to see him: seld-shown flamens
        Do press among the popular throngs and puff
        To win a vulgar station: or veil'd dames
195   Commit the war of white and damask in
        Their nicely-gawded cheeks to the wanton spoil
        Of Phoebus' burning kisses: such a pother
        As if that whatsoever god who leads him
        Were slily crept into his human powers
200   And gave him graceful posture.

SICINIUS

                                                On the sudden,
        I warrant him consul.

VOLUMNIA

> I've lived to see all my wishes come true and to possess all the things I wanted. Now there's only one thing left, which I'm sure that Rome will give you.

CORIOLANUS

> Mother, you know I'd prefer to serve the senators as a soldier than to be a public servant myself.

COMINIUS

> Let's go to the capitol!

Trumpets sounds.
All exit except **BRUTUS AND SICINIUS**.

BRUTUS

> Everyone is talking about him. People who are nearly blind wear glasses just to see him. Babbling nurses let babies cry in a tantrum while they talk about him. The kitchen maid pins her best linen around her dirty neck and climbs up the wall to see him. Storefronts are boarded up, leaden roofs covered over and all different types of people are riding their horses on top of the roofs, all trying to see him. Priests who rarely come out in public are mixed in with the common people and struggle to find a place in the crowd. Women who usually wear veils are letting their pale cheeks get sunburned. There is such mayhem that it seems like whichever god is guiding Martius has taken over his very body and given him a godly way of being.

SICINIUS

> It seems like he may become a member of the consul.

BRUTUS
                              Then our office may,
            During his power, go sleep.

SICINIUS

205   He cannot temperately transport his honours
            From where he should begin and end, but will
            Lose those he hath won.

BRUTUS
                                    In that there's comfort.

SICINIUS
                                                Doubt not

210   The commoners, for whom we stand, but they
            Upon their ancient malice will forget
            With the least cause these his new honours, which
            That he will give them make I as little question
            As he is proud to do't.

BRUTUS
                                    I heard him swear,

215   Were he to stand for consul, never would he
            Appear i' the market-place nor on him put
            The napless vesture of humility;
            Nor showing, as the manner is, his wounds

220   To the people, beg their stinking breaths.

SICINIUS
                                                'Tis right.

BRUTUS
            It was his word: O, he would miss it rather
            Than carry it but by the suit of the gentry to him,
            And the desire of the nobles.

SICINIUS
                                    I wish no better

225   Than have him hold that purpose and to put it
            In execution.

BRUTUS
                        'Tis most like he will.

BRUTUS

We'd lose power if he were admitted to the consul.

SICINIUS

He won't be able to translate his fame in battle into some other kind of victory. If he tries, he'll lose the honor he has won.

BRUTUS

That's comforting.

SICINIUS

Don't doubt the common people we represent. Their longstanding hatred for him will cause them to overlook his new honors with only the slightest provocation. And given his pride, he'll undoubtedly provoke them.

BRUTUS

I heard him declare that if he were to seek nomination to the consul, he would never appear in the marketplace wearing the traditional poor man's gown to show his humility. Nor would he show off his wounds to the people to win their approval.

SICINIUS

Is that so?

BRUTUS

He said he'd rather not be in the consul if he couldn't be admitted simply by the wishes of the common folk and the nobles.

SICINIUS

I hope he stays with that plan.

BRUTUS

Most likely, he will.

SICINIUS

It shall be to him then as our good wills,
230   A sure destruction.

BRUTUS

So it must fall out
To him or our authority. For an end.
We must suggest the people in what hatred
He still hath held them; that to's power he would
235   Have made them mules, silenced their pleaders and
Dispropertied their freedoms, holding them,
In human action and capacity,
Of no more soul nor fitness for the world
Than camels in the war, who have their provand
240   Only for bearing burdens, and sore blows
For sinking under them.

SICINIUS

This, as you say, suggested
At some time when his soaring insolence
Shall touch the people—which time shall not want,
245   If he be put upon 't; and that's as easy
As to set dogs on sheep—will be his fire
To kindle their dry stubble; and their blaze
Shall darken him for ever.

Enter a **MESSENGER**.

BRUTUS

What's the matter?

MESSENGER

250   You are sent for to the Capitol. 'Tis thought
That Martius shall be consul: I have seen
The dumb men throng to see him, and the blind
To hear him speak: matrons flung gloves,
Ladies and maids their scarfs and handkerchers,
255   Upon him as he pass'd: the nobles bended,
As to Jove's statue, and the commons made

SICINIUS

What will happen to him then will be as we wish: he'll surely lose.

BRUTUS

He must lose, or else our power will be over. We must remind the people of how much he still hates them, that if he were in charge, he'd make them work like mules, he would never listen to their requests and he'd take away their freedoms. He wouldn't recognize their humanity or their souls. He'd hold them captive like the camels who only get fed so that they can carry heavy loads in service of the war and develop sores in the process.

SICINIUS

We need to suggest this possibility to the people at a time when they're already irritated by his arrogance. There will be many occasions for this. It's as easy to get him to show off his pride as it is to get dogs to chase sheep. His pride will be like fire to their kindling wood, and their blaze will ruin him forever.

A **MESSENGER** *enters.*

BRUTUS

What's going on?

MESSENGER

The capitol sends for you. It's thought that Martius will be admitted to the consul. I saw mute people form crowds to see him and blind people to hear him speak. Married women threw their gloves to him and ladies and maids their scarfs and handkerchiefs. As he passed by, the nobles bowed to him as they would to Jupiter's statue. The common people made a shower with their caps and

A shower and thunder with their caps and shouts:
I never saw the like.

BRUTUS

                    Let's to the Capitol;
260   And carry with us ears and eyes for the time,
       But hearts for the event.

SICINIUS

                              Have with you.

                                                    Exeunt.

thunder with their shouts. I've never seen anything like it.

BRUTUS

Let's go to the Capitol and keep our eyes and ears
open for the time being, while our heart remains set on
our plan.

SICINIUS

I'm with you.

All exit.

ACT 2, SCENE 2

The same. The Capitol.
Enter two OFFICERS, *to lay cushions*

FIRST OFFICER

Come, come, they are almost here. How many stand
for consulships?

SECOND OFFICER

Three, they say: but 'tis thought of every one Coriolanus
will carry it.

FIRST OFFICER

5   That's a brave fellow; but he's vengeance proud, and
loves not the common people.

SECOND OFFICER

Faith, there had been many great men that have flattered
the people, who ne'er loved them; and there be many
that they have loved, they know not wherefore: so that, if
10   they love they know not why, they hate upon no better a
ground: therefore, for Coriolanus neither to care whether
they love or hate him manifests the true knowledge he has
in their disposition; and out of his noble carelessness lets
them plainly see't.

FIRST OFFICER

15   If he did not care whether he had their love or no, he
waved indifferently 'twixxt doing them neither good nor
harm: but he seeks their hate with greater devotion than
can render it him; and leaves nothing undone that may
fully discover him their opposite. Now, to seem to affect
20   the malice and displeasure of the people is as bad as that
which he dislikes, to flatter them for their love.

SECOND OFFICER

He hath deserved worthily of his country: and his ascent
is not by such easy degrees as those who, having been
supple and courteous to the people, bonneted, without

ACT 2, SCENE 2

The capitol.
Two OFFICERS *enter to set up seats.*

FIRST OFFICER

Hurry up. They're almost here. How many are being considered as consul?

SECOND OFFICER

Three, they say. But everyone thinks Coriolanus will get it.

FIRST OFFICER

He's a brave man, but he's too proud, and he doesn't care about the common people.

SECOND OFFICER

There have been many great men who have flattered the people but whom the people never liked, and there have been many that the people liked for unknown reasons. Since they can like someone without knowing why, at least when they dislike someone, it's for an equally vague reason. So for Coriolanus not to care whether they like him or not shows that he actually knows them quite well, and out of his own indifference to public opinion, he lets them know that he doesn't care.

FIRST OFFICER

If he didn't care whether or not he had their support, he would be indifferent to either doing them good or harm. But he provokes their hatred with more intensity than they can hate him with in return. He has done everything possible for them to see him as their enemy. However, to pretend to desire the ill will of the people is as bad as flattering them for their approval—something he would never do.

SECOND OFFICER

He has served his country honorably and his route to prominence has not been nearly as easy as those who,

25 any further deed to have them at all into their estimation
and report: but he hath so planted his honours in their
eyes, and his actions in their hearts, that for their tongues
to be silent, and not confess so much, were a kind of
ingrateful injury; to report otherwise, were a malice, that,
30 giving itself the lie, would pluck reproof and rebuke from
every ear that heard it.

FIRST OFFICER

No more of him; he is a worthy man: make way, they
are coming.

*A sennet. Enter, with actors before them, the patricians and
the tribunes of the people, CORIOLANUS, MENENIUS, COMINIUS
the consul. The patricians sit. SICINIUS and BRUTUS take their
places by themselves. CORIOLANUS stands.*

MENENIUS

Having determined of the Volsces and
35 To send for Titus Lartius, it remains,
As the main point of this our after-meeting,
To gratify his noble service that
Hath thus stood for his country: therefore, please you,
Most reverend and grave elders, to desire
40 The present consul, and last general
In our well-found successes, to report
A little of that worthy work perform'd
By Martius Caius Coriolanus, whom
We met here both to thank and to remember
45 With honours like himself.

CORIOLANUS sits.

FIRST SENATOR

Speak, good Cominius:
Leave nothing out for length, and make us think
Rather our state's defective for requital
Than we to stretch it out.

having been lenient and kind to the people, only tipped
their hats to get ahead. But he has boasted in their faces
so much about his fame and his actions, that if they don't
pay attention to this, they would be harming themselves.
If they lie about his prideful behavior, no one would
believe them. Everyone would say otherwise.

FIRST OFFICER

Stop talking about him. He's a worthy man. Make way.
They're coming.

Trumpets sound. COMINIUS *the consul,* MENENIUS,
CORIOLANUS, SENATORS, SICINIUS, *and* BRUTUS *enter,
with attendants going in before them. The Senators take their
places.* SICINIUS *and* BRUTUS *take their places by themselves.*
CORIOLANUS *stands.*

MENENIUS

Once we decide what to do about the Volsces and send
for Titus Lartius, the main point of this meeting is still
to reward his noble service in defending his country.
Therefore, most respected and honorable elders, the
present consul and the general in our victorious battles
desires to report a little of the worthy work performed by
Martius Caius Coriolanus, whom we have invited here
both to thank and to honor.

CORIOLANUS *sits*

FIRST SENATOR

Speak as long as you need, good Cominius. Leave
nothing out. Better that he think we don't have the
resources to reward to him than that we don't have the
patience to listen to the full report.

50   (*to the tribunes*) Masters o' the people,
        We do request your kindest ears, and after,
        Your loving motion toward the common body,
        To yield what passes here.

SICINIUS
                                        We are convented
55   Upon a pleasing treaty, and have hearts
        Inclinable to honour and advance
        The theme of our assembly.

BRUTUS
                                        Which the rather
        We shall be blest to do, if he remember
60   A kinder value of the people than
        He hath hereto prized them at.

MENENIUS
                                        That's off, that's off!
        I would you rather had been silent. Please you
        To hear Cominius speak?

BRUTUS
65   Most willingly;
        But yet my caution was more pertinent
        Than the rebuke you give it.

MENENIUS
                                        He loves your people
        But tie him not to be their bedfellow.
70   Worthy Cominius, speak.

                        CORIOLANUS *rises and offers to go away.*
                                        Nay, keep your place.

FIRST SENATOR
        Sit, Coriolanus; never shame to hear
        What you have nobly done.

CORIOLANUS
                                        Your Honours pardon:
75   I had rather have my wounds to heal again
        Than hear say how I got them.

(To the tribunes) Representatives of the people, we request
you to listen kindly, and afterward to convince the people
to agree to what we suggest.

SICINIUS

> We've come here to consider this question, and
> we're inclined to honor and advance the cause of
> our constituents.

BRUTUS

> Which we'll happily do, and soon, if he can remember to
> value the people more highly than he has previously.

MENENIUS

> That's not the point. I wish you had been silent. Please,
> will you let Cominius speak?

BRUTUS

> Most willingly. But my caution was more important than
> you realize.

MENENIUS

> He cares about the common people. Just don't
> expect him to be closely involved with them. Worthy
> Cominius, speak.

> > CORIOLANUS *tries to get up and leave.*

> No, stay where you are.

FIRST SENATOR

> Sit, Coriolanus. Never be embarrassed to hear of your
> noble deeds.

CORIOLANUS

> I'm sorry, your honor. I'd rather let my wounds heal than
> hear how I got them.

BRUTUS

                                    Sir, I hope

My words disbench'd you not.

CORIOLANUS

                                 No, sir: yet oft,

80   When blows have made me stay, I fled from words.

You soothed not, therefore hurt not: but your people,

I love them as they weigh.

MENENIUS

                          Pray now, sit down.

CORIOLANUS

I had rather have one scratch my head i' the sun

85   When the alarum were struck than idly sit

To hear my nothings monster'd.

                                    Coriolanus exits.

MENENIUS

                        Masters of the people,

Your multiplying spawn how can he flatter—

That's thousand to one good one—when you now see

90   He had rather venture all his limbs for honour

Than one on's ears to hear it. Proceed, Cominius.

COMINIUS

I shall lack voice: the deeds of Coriolanus

Should not be utter'd feebly. It is held

That valour is the chiefest virtue, and

95   Most dignifies the haver: if it be,

The man I speak of cannot in the world

Be singly counterpoised. At sixteen years,

When Tarquin made a head for Rome, he fought

Beyond the mark of others: our then dictator,

100   Whom with all praise I point at, saw him fight,

When with his Amazonian chin he drove

The bristled lips before him. He bestrid

An o'er-press'd Roman and i' the consul's view

BRUTUS

> Sir, I hope my words didn't cause you to get up.

CORIOLANUS

> No, sir. While I don't run from fights, I do often run from praise. But you didn't flatter me, so I wasn't offended. But the people you represent are worth so little, so I care so little about them.

MENENIUS

> Please, sit down.

CORIOLANUS

> I'd rather let someone scratch my head in the sun when the trumpet summons me to battle than sit here and listen to my small deeds be over-embellished.

> *Coriolanus exits.*

MENENIUS

> Representatives of the people, your constituents reproduce all the time, and there's only one good man among every thousand of them—how can he flatter them? You see now he'd rather risk his whole life for honor than risk one of his ears to hear about it. Go on, Cominius.

COMINIUS

> I won't say much. The deeds of Coriolanus shouldn't be spoken of lightly. It's well known that courage is the highest virtue and brings the highest dignity to whoever has it. And if that's true, there's no one in the world who is more dignified than the man I speak of. At age sixteen, when Tarquin attacked Rome, his fighting exceeded everyone else's. Our former leader, whom I reference with all praise, saw him fight victoriously against adults when he was still young and had a beardless chin. He protected the overwhelmed Romans and as the consul

Slew three opposers: Tarquin's self he met,
105   And struck him on his knee: in that day's feats,
When he might act the woman in the scene,
He proved best man i' the field, and for his meed
Was brow-bound with the oak. His pupil age
Man-enter'd thus, he waxed like a sea,
110   And in the brunt of seventeen battles since
He lurch'd all swords of the garland. For this last,
Before and in Corioles, let me say,
I cannot speak him home: he stopp'd the fliers;
And by his rare example made the coward
115   Turn terror into sport: as weeds before
A vessel under sail, so men obey'd
And fell below his stem: his sword, death's stamp,
Where it did mark, it took; from face to foot
He was a thing of blood, whose every motion
120   Was timed with dying cries: alone he enter'd
The mortal gate of the city, which he painted
With shunless destiny; aidless came off,
And with a sudden reinforcement struck
Corioles like a planet: now all's his:
125   When, by and by, the din of war gan pierce
His ready sense; then straight his doubled spirit
Re-quicken'd what in flesh was fatigate,
And to the battle came he; where he did
Run reeking o'er the lives of men, as if
130   'Twere a perpetual spoil: and till we call'd
Both field and city ours, he never stood
To ease his breast with panting.

MENENIUS
                                        Worthy man!

FIRST SENATOR
He cannot but with measure fit the honours
135   Which we devise him.

watched, he defeated three enemies. He fought Tarquin himself and brought him to his knees. In that day of fighting, when he was young enough to play a woman on stage, he proved to be the best man in the field, and he was rewarded with a garland of oak. He entered into manhood, though he was still a boy, with the force of a rising tide. He has led the attack in seventeen battles since then, and he has triumphed over his fellow soldiers every time. As for this last battle, outside of and within Corioles, I have no words to describe what he did. He stopped the Roman deserters and by his rare example made these cowards overcome their fear and become warriors. The men obeyed and fell beneath his prow like waves beneath a sailboat. Wherever he swung his sword, he marked the sign of death. From head to toe he was covered in blood, and his every motion was followed by dying cries. He entered the deadly gate of the city alone, and he painted it with the blood of their inevitable destiny. Without help, he retreated, but with a sudden burst of energy he attacked Corioles with the force of a planet. Then the city was all his. After a while, as the noise of war began to wear him down, his spirit reinvigorated his tired body, and he came back to the battle and ran furiously at the enemy, as if it were an endless slaughter. He never stopped to catch his breath until both the field and city were ours.

MENENIUS

Worthy man!

FIRST SENATOR

He definitely measures up to the honors we have for him.

COMINIUS

                      Our spoils he kick'd at,
And look'd upon things precious as they were
The common muck of the world: he covets less
Than misery itself would give, rewards

140   His deeds with doing them, and is content
To spend the time to end it.

MENENIUS

                          He's right noble:
Let him be call'd for.

FIRST SENATOR

Call Coriolanus.

OFFICER

145   He doth appear.

Re-enter **CORIOLANUS**.

MENENIUS

The senate, Coriolanus, are well pleased
To make thee consul.

CORIOLANUS

                    I do owe them still
My life and services.

MENENIUS

150   It then remains
That you do speak to the people.

CORIOLANUS

                      I do beseech you,
Let me o'erleap that custom, for I cannot
Put on the gown, stand naked and entreat them,

155   For my wounds' sake, to give their suffrage: please you
That I may pass this doing.

SICINIUS

                    Sir, the people
Must have their voices; neither will they bate
One jot of ceremony.

COMINIUS

> He rejected our spoils and looked at precious things as if they were the common muck of the world. He doesn't desire anything. To him, doing his deeds is its own reward, and he's happy to spend the time doing the job well.

MENENIUS

> He's very noble. Let's call him here.

FIRST SENATOR

> Call Coriolanus.

OFFICER

> Here he is.

> *CORIOLANUS re-enters.*

MENENIUS

> Coriolanus, the Senate is very happy to admit you to the consul.

CORIOLANUS

> I'll always owe them my life and services.

MENENIUS

> All that remains is for you to speak to the people.

CORIOLANUS

> I beg you, let me skip that custom. I can't put on the gown, stand without an undershirt, and show off my wounds just so they'll vote for me. Please let me forgo this.

SICINIUS

> Sir, the people must have their say, and they won't leave out one bit of the ceremony.

MENENIUS

160   (*to* CORIOLANUS)   Put them not to't:
Pray you, go fit you to the custom and
Take to you, as your predecessors have,
Your honour with your form.

CORIOLANUS

It is apart
165   That I shall blush in acting, and might well
Be taken from the people.

BRUTUS

(*to* SICINUS)   Mark you that?

CORIOLANUS

To brag unto them, "thus I did, and thus!";
Show them the unaching scars which I should hide,
170   As if I had received them for the hire
Of their breath only!

MENENIUS

Do not stand upon't.
We recommend to you, tribunes of the people,
Our purpose to them: and to our noble consul
175   Wish we all joy and honour.

SENATORS

To Coriolanus come all joy and honour!
Flourish of cornets. Exeunt all but SICINIUS *and* BRUTUS.

BRUTUS

You see how he intends to use the people.

SICINIUS

May they perceive's intent! He will require them,
As if he did contemn what he requested
180   Should be in them to give.

BRUTUS

Come, we'll inform them
Of our proceedings here: on the marketplace,
I know, they do attend us.

Exeunt.

MENENIUS

> (*to* CORIOLANUS) Don't fight them on this. Go through with this custom and stand honorably as your predecessors have.

CORIOLANUS

> I'll blush as I play this part. The people will be deceived.

BRUTUS

> (*to* SICINIUS) Did you hear that?

CORIOLANUS

> To brag of the things I've done and show them my old scars, which I should hide—as if I'd received them only for the people to gasp at!

MENENIUS

> Don't insist on this. Tribunes of the people, we ask that you recommend our proposal to the people. And to our noble consul wish we all joy and honor.

SENATORS

> May all joy and honor come to Coriolanus!

> *Sound of trumpets.*
> *Everyone exits except* SICINIUS *and* BRUTUS

BRUTUS

> You see how he intends to use the people.

SICINIUS

> May they know his intentions! He'll ask for their support even though he hates that it's in their power to give it.

BRUTUS

> Let's go inform them of what's happened here. I know they're waiting for us in the marketplace.

> *All exit.*

ACT 2, SCENE 3

The same. The Forum.
Enter seven or eight CITIZENS.

FIRST CITIZEN
Once, if he do require our voices, we ought not to
deny him.

SECOND CITIZEN
We may, sir, if we will.

THIRD CITIZEN
We have power in ourselves to do it, but it is a power that
5   we have no power to do; for if he show us his wounds
and tell us his deeds, we are to put our tongues into those
wounds and speak for them; so, if he tell us his noble
deeds, we must also tell him our noble acceptance of
them. Ingratitude is monstrous, and for the multitude to
10   be ingrateful, were to make a monster of the multitude: of
the which we being members, should bring ourselves to
be monstrous members.

FIRST CITIZEN
And to make us no better thought of, a little help will
serve; for once we stood up about the corn, he himself
15   stuck not to call us the many-headed multitude.

THIRD CITIZEN
We have been called so of many; not that our heads are
some brown, some black, some auburn, some bald, but
that our wits are so diversely coloured: and truly I think if
all our wits were to issue out of one skull, they would fly
20   east, west, north, south, and their consent of one direct
way should be at once to all the points o' the compass.

SECOND CITIZEN
Think you so? Which way do you judge my wit
would fly?

ACT 2, SCENE 3

The Roman marketplace.
Seven or eight CITIZENS *enter.*

FIRST CITIZEN

If and when he asks for our votes, we shouldn't deny him.

SECOND CITIZEN

We can deny him, sir, if we want to.

THIRD CITIZEN

We have the right to deny him, but it wouldn't be the right thing to do. If he shows us his wounds and tells us of his deeds, we must honor those wounds with our votes. And if he tells us of his noble deeds, we must then tell him of our gratitude. Ingratitude is monstrous, and for the people to be seen as ungrateful would make us into monsters.

FIRST CITIZEN

And it wouldn't take much to make us worse thought of. When we complained about the corn, he didn't hesitate to call us an unstable mass of people.

THIRD CITIZEN

Many people have called us that. Not because some of us have brown hair, some black, some blond and some bald, but because our opinions are so diverse. I truly think that if all our opinions were to come from one mind, they would go east, west, north, and south. All they could agree on would be to go in different directions.

SECOND CITIZEN

Do you think so? Which way do you think my opinion would go?

THIRD CITIZEN

25   Nay, your wit will not so soon out as another man's will;
'tis strongly wedged up in a block-head, but if it were at
liberty, 'twould, sure, southward.

SECOND CITIZEN

Why that way?

THIRD CITIZEN

To lose itself in a fog, where being three parts melted
30   away with rotten dews, the fourth would return for
conscience sake, to help to get thee a wife.

SECOND CITIZEN

You are never without your tricks: you may, you may.

THIRD CITIZEN

Are you all resolved to give your voices? But that's no
matter, the greater part carries it. I say, if he would incline
35   to the people, there was never a worthier man.

Enter CORIOLANUS *in a gown of humility, with* MENENIUS.

Here he comes, and in the gown of humility: mark his
behavior. We are not to stay all together, but to come by
him where he stands, by ones, by twos, and by threes.
He's to make his requests by particulars; wherein every
40   one of us has a single honour, in giving him our own
voices with our own tongues: therefore follow me, and I
direct you how you shall go by him.

ALL

Content, content.

Exeunt CITIZENS.

MENENIUS

O sir, you are not right: have you not known
45   The worthiest men have done't?

THIRD CITIZEN

You're stubborn, so your opinion will stay stuck inside you until another man's will expresses itself first. If yours could come out, though, it would surely go south.

SECOND CITIZEN

Why that way?

THIRD CITIZEN

To lose itself in the plague-ridden air. Three-quarters of it would melt away in the contagious dew, and the remaining quarter would have a conscience and return to help you get a wife.

SECOND CITIZEN

You're never without your jokes. It's okay—you can laugh at me.

THIRD CITIZEN

Are you all ready to vote? It doesn't actually matter, since the majority vote wins. If only he cared about the people, he would be the most deserving man there ever was.

CORIOLANUS, *in a gown of humility, and* MENENIUS *enter.*

Here he comes, wearing the gown of humility. Watch his behavior. We're not supposed to all stay together but rather go up to him where he's standing, either alone or in groups of two or three. He's supposed to make his request to us individually, and each of us has the separate honor of giving him our own vote in our own voice. Follow me. I'll show you how to go up to him.

ALL

Okay, okay.

The CITIZENS *exit.*

MENENIUS

Oh, sir, you don't understand. Don't you know that the most honorable men have done this?

CORIOLANUS
                                     What must I say?
"I Pray, sir"—Plague upon't! I cannot bring
My tongue to such a pace:—"Look, sir, my wounds!
I got them in my country's service, when
50   Some certain of your brethren roar'd and ran
From the noise of our own drums."

MENENIUS
                                     O me, the gods!
You must not speak of that: you must desire them
To think upon you.

CORIOLANUS
55   Think upon me? hang 'em!
I would they would forget me, like the virtues
Which our divines lose by 'em.

MENENIUS
                                     You'll mar all:
I'll leave you: pray you, speak to 'em, I pray you,
60   In wholesome manner.

                              MENENIUS *exits.*

CORIOLANUS
                              Bid them wash their faces
And keep their teeth clean.

Re-enter two of the CITIZENS.

                              So, here comes a brace.

Re-enter a third CITIZEN

You know the cause, sir, of my standing here.

THIRD CITIZEN
65   We do, sir; tell us what hath brought you to't.

CORIOLANUS
Mine own desert.

CORIOLANUS

What am I supposed to say? "Please, sir"—Curse that!
I can't force myself to say such a thing. "Look at my
wounds, sir. I got them while serving my country, while
men who were undoubtedly your brothers cried and ran
away from the battle."

MENENIUS

Oh, gods! You can't talk about that. You need to get them
to think well of you.

CORIOLANUS

Think well of me! Hang them! I wish they would forget
me, like they have forgotten the virtues that the gods
didn't sufficiently instill in them.

MENENIUS

You'll ruin everything. I'm leaving now. Please, keep it
clean with them.

MENENIUS exits.

CORIOLANUS

I'll ask them to wash their faces and brush their teeth.

Two CITIZENS re-enter.

So, here comes a pair.

A third CITIZEN re-enters.

You know why I'm standing here.

THIRD CITIZEN

We do, sir. Tell us what brought you here.

CORIOLANUS

It's what I deserve.

SECOND CITIZEN
　　Your own desert!
CORIOLANUS
　　Ay, but not mine own desire.
THIRD CITIZEN
　　How not your own desire?
CORIOLANUS
70　　No, sir, 'twas never my desire yet to trouble the
　　poor with begging.
THIRD CITIZEN
　　You must think, if we give you any thing, we hope to
　　gain by you.
CORIOLANUS
　　Well then, I pray, your price o' the consulship?

FIRST CITIZEN
75　　The price is to ask it kindly.
CORIOLANUS
　　Kindly! Sir, I pray, let me ha't: I have wounds to
　　show you, which shall be yours in private. Your
　　good voice, sir; what say you?
SECOND CITIZEN
　　You shall ha' it, worthy sir.
CORIOLANUS
80　　A match, sir. There's in all two worthy voices
　　begged. I have your alms: adieu.
THIRD CITIZEN
　　(*to the other* CITIZENS) But this is something odd.
SECOND CITIZEN
　　An 'twere to give again,—but 'tis no matter.
　　　　　　　　　　　　Exeunt the three CITIZENS.

Re-enter two other CITIZENS.

SECOND CITIZEN

It's what you deserve!

CORIOLANUS

Yes, but it's not what I desire.

THIRD CITIZEN

You don't desire it?

CORIOLANUS

No, sir, I never desired to trouble the poor with begging.

THIRD CITIZEN

You must think that if we give you something, we hope to get something from you.

CORIOLANUS

Well then, tell me: what will it cost for you to give me the consulship?

FIRST CITIZEN

The price is to ask for it kindly.

CORIOLANUS

Please, sir, kindly let me have it. I have wounds to show you, which I'll show you in private. Your vote, sir, what do you say?

SECOND CITIZEN

You'll get my vote, worthy sir.

CORIOLANUS

It's a deal, sir. That's two deserving votes I've secured. Thank you for your charity. Goodbye.

THIRD CITIZEN

(to the other CITIZENS*)* This is strange.

SECOND CITIZEN

If I could vote again, but never mind.

The three CITIZENS *exit.*

Two other CITIZENS *re-enter.*

CORIOLANUS

Pray you now, if it may stand with the tune of your
85   voices that I may be consul, I have here the
customary gown.

FOURTH CITIZEN

You have deserved nobly of your country, and you
have not deserved nobly.

CORIOLANUS

Your enigma?

FOURTH CITIZEN

90   You have been a scourge to her enemies, you have
been a rod to her friends; you have not indeed loved
the common people.

CORIOLANUS

You should account me the more virtuous that I have
not been common in my love. I will, sir, flatter my
95   sworn brother, the people, to earn a dearer estimation of
them; 'tis a condition they account gentle: and since the
wisdom of their choice is rather to have my hat than my
heart, I will practice the insinuating nod and be off to
them most counterfeitly; that is, sir, I will counterfeit the
100 bewitchment of some popular man and give it bountiful
to the desirers. Therefore, beseech you, I may be consul.

FIFTH CITIZEN

We hope to find you our friend; and therefore give
you our voices heartily.

FOURTH CITIZEN

You have received many wounds for your country.

CORIOLANUS

105 I will not seal your knowledge with showing them.
I will make much of your voices, and so trouble you
no further.

BOTH CITIZENS

The gods give you joy, sir, heartily!

Exeunt.

CORIOLANUS

> I ask if you would please vote for me, since I am wearing the customary gown.

FOURTH CITIZEN

> You've served your country nobly, but you aren't deserving.

CORIOLANUS

> What do you mean?

FOURTH CITIZEN

> You've defeated her enemies and you've protected her friends, but you haven't loved the common people.

CORIOLANUS

> You should consider me virtuous because I don't give my love away easily. Sir, I'll flatter my sworn brothers, the people, so they'll think well of me. It's a custom they consider noble. And since they'd rather decide based on what hat I'm wearing than on who I am, I'll practice taking off my hat and bowing insincerely. That is to say, sir, I'll pretend to be enchanted by them, as some popular men do, and give my false admiration plentifully to those who desire it. So I ask you, may I be consul?

FIFTH CITIZEN

> We hope you'll be our ally, so we happily vote for you.

FOURTH CITIZEN

> You've been wounded many times serving your country.

CORIOLANUS

> I won't confirm what you already know by showing my wounds to you. I'll just take your votes and not trouble you further.

BOTH CITIZENS

> May the gods give you much joy, sir!

> > *The* CITIZENS *exit.*

CORIOLANUS

Most sweet voices!
110 Better it is to die, better to starve,
Than crave the hire which first we do deserve.
Why in this woolvish toge should I stand here,
To beg of Hob and Dick, that do appear,
Their needless vouches? Custom calls me to't:
115 What custom wills, in all things should we do't?
The dust on antique time would lie unswept,
And mountainous error be too highly heapt
For truth to o'erpeer. Rather than fool it so,
Let the high office and the honour go
120 To one that would do thus. I am half through;
The one part suffer'd, the other will I do.

Enter three CITIZENS *more.*

Here come more voices.
Your voices: for your voices I have fought;
Watch'd for your voices; for your voices bear
125 Of wounds two dozen odd; battles thrice six
I have seen and heard of; for your voices have
Done many things, some less, some more your voices:
Indeed I would be consul.

SIXTH CITIZEN

He has done nobly, and cannot go without any honest
130 man's voice.

SEVENTH CITIZEN

Therefore let him be consul: the gods give him joy,
and make him good friend to the people!

ALL CITIZENS

Amen, amen. God save thee, noble consul!

Exeunt.

CORIOLANUS

Worthy voices!

CORIOLANUS

Most sweet voters! It's better to die, better to starve, than to beg to be chosen for a position you already deserve. Why must I stand here in this hypocritical toga and beg the commoners for their meaningless approval, which I shouldn't need? Custom forces me to do it, and what custom requires, we must do. It's an ancient tradition that has gone on for so long that no one can see that it's a huge mistake. I wish I didn't have to play the fool, but the honor of the consulship goes to he who will. I'm halfway done. I'll do the other half.

Three more CITIZENS *enter.*

Here come more votes. Your votes: I have fought for your votes and stayed out on watch for your votes. For your votes I have been wounded more than two dozen times and been in thirty-six battles. For your votes, I have seen and heard many things and done some things less and some things more—all for your votes, so I can be in the consul.

SIXTH CITIZEN

He has served nobly and must win any honest man's vote.

SEVENTH CITIZEN

Therefore let him be the consul. May the gods give him joy and make him be good to the people!

ALL CITIZENS

Amen, amen. God save thee, noble consul

CITIZENS *all exit.*

CORIOLANUS

Worthy voters!

Re-enter MENENIUS, *with* BRUTUS *and* SICINIUS.

MENENIUS

135   You have stood your limitation; and the tribunes
Endue you with the people's voice: remains
That, in the official marks invested, you
Anon do meet the senate.

CORIOLANUS

                      Is this done?

SICINIUS

140   The custom of request you have discharged:
The people do admit you, and are summon'd
To meet anon, upon your approbation.

CORIOLANUS

Where? at the senate house?

SICINIUS

                    There, Coriolanus.

CORIOLANUS

145   May I change these garments?

SICINIUS

                      You may, sir.

CORIOLANUS

That I'll straight do; and, knowing myself again,
Repair to the senate house.

MENENIUS

I'll keep you company. Will you along?

BRUTUS

150   We stay here for the people.

SICINIUS

                  Fare you well.

Exeunt CORIOLANUS *and* MENENIUS.

He has it now, and by his looks methink
'Tis warm at 's heart.

BRUTUS

              With a proud heart he wore
His humble weeds. Will you dismiss the people?

MENENIUS *re-enters, with* BRUTUS *and* SICINIUS.

MENENIUS

> You've stood here for the time required, and the tribunes approve you with the people's endorsement. All that remains is to make it official. We must go now to the senators.

CORIOLANUS

> It's over?

SICINIUS

> You've performed the required custom, and the people admit you to the consul. Go meet the senators so they can approve your election.

CORIOLANUS

> Where? At the Senate house?

SICINIUS

> Yes, Coriolanus.

CORIOLANUS

> May I change out of these clothes?

SICINIUS

> You may, sir.

CORIOLANUS

> I'll do that first, and once I feel like myself again, I'll go to the Senate house.

MENENIUS

> I'll keep you company. Will you come, too?

BRUTUS

> We'll stay here with the people.

SICINIUS

> Good luck.

> > > CORIOLANUS *and* MENENIUS *exit.*

> He has the consulship now, and he looks happy about it.

BRUTUS

> He wore the gown of humility, but his heart was still proud. Will you let the people's vote stand?

Re-enter the CITIZENS.

SICINIUS

155   How now, my masters, have you chose this man?

FIRST CITIZEN

He has our voices, sir.

BRUTUS

We pray the gods he may deserve your loves.

SECOND CITIZEN

Amen, sir: to my poor unworthy notice,
He mock'd us when he begg'd our voices.

THIRD CITIZEN

160   Certainly, he flouted us downright.

FIRST CITIZEN

No, 'tis his kind of speech: he did not mock us.

SECOND CITIZEN

Not one amongst us, save yourself, but says
He used us scornfully: he should have show'd us
His marks of merit, wounds received for's country.

SICINIUS

165   Why, so he did, I am sure.

CITIZENS

No, no; no man saw 'em.

THIRD CITIZEN

He said he had wounds, which he could show in private;
And with his hat, thus waving it in scorn,
"I would be consul," says he: "aged custom,
170   But by your voices, will not so permit me;
Your voices therefore." When we granted that,
Here was "I thank you for your voices: thank you:
Your most sweet voices: now you have left your voices,
I have no further with you." Was not this mockery?

SICINIUS

175   Why either were you ignorant to see't,
Or, seeing it, of such childish friendliness
To yield your voices?

CITIZENS *re-enter.*

SICINIUS

How are you, good people? Have you chosen this man?

FIRST CITIZEN

He has our votes, sir.

BRUTUS

We pray to the gods that he deserves your favor.

SECOND CITIZEN

Amen, sir. I'm not certain, but I think he mocked us while asking for our votes.

THIRD CITIZEN

He expressed his contempt for us in no uncertain terms.

FIRST CITIZEN

No, that's just the way he speaks. He didn't mock us.

SECOND CITIZEN

All of us, except you, say he used us scornfully. He should have showed us his marks of merit, the wounds he received for his country.

SICINIUS

I'm sure he showed you.

CITIZENS

No, no. No one saw them.

THIRD CITIZEN

He said he had wounds he could show in private. He waved his hat scornfully and said, "I should be the consul but because of this ancient custom, I can't be without your votes, so give me your votes." When we gave them to him, he said, "I thank you for your votes. Thank you. Your most sweet votes, now that you've given me your votes, I have no further use for you." Isn't that mockery?

SICINIUS

You were either too ignorant to see it, or if you did see it, you were too childish and accommodating to deny him your vote.

BRUTUS

Could you not have told him
As you were lesson'd, when he had no power,
180   But was a petty servant to the state,
He was your enemy, ever spake against
Your liberties and the charters that you bear
I' the body of the weal; and now, arriving
A place of potency and sway o' the state,
185   If he should still malignantly remain
Fast foe to the plebeii, your voices might
Be curses to yourselves. You should have said
That as his worthy deeds did claim no less
Than what he stood for, so his gracious nature
190   Would think upon you for your voices and
Translate his malice towards you into love,
Standing your friendly lord.

SICINIUS

Thus to have said,
As you were fore-advised, had touch'd his spirit
195   And tried his inclination; from him pluck'd
Either his gracious promise, which you might,
As cause had call'd you up, have held him to
Or else it would have gall'd his surly nature,
Which easily endures not article
200   Tying him to aught; so putting him to rage,
You should have ta'en the advantage of his choler
And pass'd him unelected.

BRUTUS

Did you perceive
He did solicit you in free contempt
205   When he did need your loves, and do you think
That his contempt shall not be bruising to you,
When he hath power to crush? Why, had your bodies
No heart among you? or had you tongues to cry
Against the rectorship of judgment?

NO FEAR SHAKESPEARE

BRUTUS

> Couldn't you have told him as you were instructed?
> When he had no power and was only a petty servant
> of the state, he was your enemy. He has always spoken
> against your freedom and the legal privileges you
> have. Now that he's arriving in a position of power and
> influence on the state, if he remains such an evil enemy
> to the people, you might have cause to curse yourself for
> giving him your votes. You should have said that while
> his acts of bravery do entitle him to the consulship, he
> should also be gracious and think well of you for giving
> him your approval. He should transform his hatred
> toward you into love and become your political advocate.

SICINIUS

> If you'd said that, as you were advised ahead of time,
> it would have touched his spirit and changed his
> inclination. You might have gotten a gracious promise
> from him, which you could have held him to when you
> needed it. Or else it would have provoked his angry
> nature, which is easily done, and he would have gone into
> a rage. You could have used his anger as reason not to vote
> for him.

BRUTUS

> Didn't you notice that he asked for your vote in blatant
> contempt even when he needed your approval? So don't
> you think that his contempt will harm you when he
> has power to exercise? Didn't you have any courage?
> Couldn't you cry out against the status quo?

SICINIUS

210   Have you ere now denied the asker? and now again
Of him that did not ask, but mock, bestow
Your sued-for tongues?

THIRD CITIZEN

                          He's not confirm'd;
We may deny him yet.

SECOND CITIZEN

215   And will deny him:
I'll have five hundred voices of that sound.

FIRST CITIZEN

I twice five hundred and their friends to piece 'em.

BRUTUS

Get you hence instantly, and tell those friends,
They have chose a consul that will from them take
220   Their liberties; make them of no more voice
Than dogs that are as often beat for barking
As therefore kept to do so.

SICINIUS

                      Let them assemble,
And on a safer judgment all revoke
225   Your ignorant election; enforce his pride,
And his old hate unto you; besides, forget not
With what contempt he wore the humble weed,
How in his suit he scorn'd you; but your loves,
Thinking upon his services, took from you
230   The apprehension of his present portance,
Which most gibingly, ungravely, he did fashion
After the inveterate hate he bears you.

BRUTUS

                              Lay
A fault on us, your tribunes; that we laboured,
235   No impediment between, but that you must
Cast your election on him.

SICINIUS

Haven't you ever refused to vote for someone? And now you give your vote to someone who didn't even ask for it but mocked you instead?

THIRD CITIZEN

He's not confirmed. We can still deny him.

SECOND CITIZEN

And we will deny him. I'll get five hundred people to vote against him.

FIRST CITIZEN

I'll get a thousand people and their friends, too.

BRUTUS

Go do it immediately, and tell those friends that they've chosen someone for the consul who will take away their freedoms and give them no more voice than dogs have that are repeatedly beaten for barking even though their job is to bark.

SICINIUS

Let them come together and make a wiser judgment to revoke your ignorant election. Emphasize his pride and his longstanding hatred of you. And don't forget the contempt with which he wore the gown of humility and how in his quest for your votes, he scorned you. Your admiration of his past service kept you from noticing of his present way of being, which was insulting and inappropriate and reflective of the hatred he feels for you.

BRUTUS

Blame us, your tribunes. Say that we pushed you not to let these obstacles stop you from voting for him, but that you must repeal your election of him.

SICINIUS

                                  Say, you chose him
More after our commandment than as guided
By your own true affections, and that your minds,
240   Preoccupied with what you rather must do
Than what you should, made you against the grain
To voice him consul: lay the fault on us.

BRUTUS

Ay, spare us not. Say we read lectures to you.
How youngly he began to serve his country,
245   How long continued, and what stock he springs of,
The noble house o' the Martians, from whence came
That Ancus Martius, Numa's daughter's son,
Who, after great Hostilius, here was king;
Of the same house Publius and Quintus were,
250   That our best water brought by conduits hither;
And Censorinus, that was so surnamed,
And nobly named so, twice being censor,
Was his great ancestor.

SICINIUS

                            One thus descended,
255   That hath besides well in his person wrought
To be set high in place, we did commend
To your remembrances: but you have found,
Scaling his present bearing with his past,
That he's your fixed enemy, and revoke
260   Your sudden approbation.

BRUTUS

                        Say, you ne'er had done't—
Harp on that still—but by our putting on;
And presently, when you have drawn your number,
Repair to the Capitol.

ALL

265   We will so: almost all
Repent in their election.

                              Exeunt CITIZENS.

SICINIUS

> Say that you chose him based more on our instructions
> than on your own true feelings, and that because you
> were preoccupied with what you thought was expected
> of you, you went against your own interest by voting him
> consul. Lay the fault on us.

BRUTUS

> Indeed, don't spare us. Say we told you all about him,
> about how young he was when he began to serve his
> country and how long he has done so, about the noble
> family he comes from—the same family as Ancus
> Martius, Numa's daughter's son, who was king after
> great Hostilius. He's from the same family as Publius
> and Quintus, the ones who built our best water conduits.
> And his great ancestor, suitably named Censorinus, was
> chosen twice as censor by the people.

SICINIUS

> We asked you to remember that he's a man descended
> from a famous family, who also has earned his own
> high praise. But you have found, weighing his present
> behavior against his past, that he's definitely your enemy,
> and you repeal your hasty approval.

BRUTUS

> Say that you never would have done it—emphasize
> that—if we hadn't put you up to it. And then, when you
> have enough people on your side, go to the capitol.

ALL

> We will. Almost everyone regrets the vote they gave.
>
> *The* CITIZENS *exit.*

BRUTUS

> Let them go on;
> This mutiny were better put in hazard,
> Than stay, past doubt, for greater:
> If, as his nature is, he fall in rage
> With their refusal, both observe and answer
> The vantage of his anger.

SICINIUS

> To the Capitol, come:
> We will be there before the stream o' the people;
> And this shall seem, as partly 'tis, their own,
> Which we have goaded onward.

Exeunt.

BRUTUS

Let them go on their own. Better to risk this rebellion than wait for the undoubtedly bigger one that would come later. If, his nature being what it is, he goes into a rage over their refusal, both watch for and take advantage of his anger.

SICINIUS

Let's go to the capitol. We'll be there before the uprising of the people. And it will appear to be their own initiative, which it partially is, although we urged them into action.

All exit.

ACT THREE

SCENE 1

Rome. A street.
Cornets. Enter CORIOLANUS, MENENIUS, *all the Gentry,*
COMINIUS, TITUS LARTIUS, *and other Senators.*

CORIOLANUS
Tullus Aufidius then had made new head?

LARTIUS
He had, my lord; and that it was which caused
Our swifter composition.

CORIOLANUS
280   So then the Volsces stand but as at first,
Ready, when time shall prompt them, to make road.
Upon's again.

COMINIUS
          They are worn, lord consul, so,
That we shall hardly in our ages see
285   Their banners wave again.

CORIOLANUS
          Saw you Aufidius?

LARTIUS
On safe-guard he came to me; and did curse
Against the Volsces, for they had so vilely
Yielded the town: he is retired to Antium.

CORIOLANUS
290   Spoke he of me?

LARTIUS
        He did, my lord.

CORIOLANUS
          How? what?

LARTIUS
How often he had met you, sword to sword;
That of all things upon the earth he hated

ACT THREE
SCENE 1

A street in Rome.
Trumpets sound. CORIOLANUS, MENENIUS, *all the noblemen,*
COMINIUS, TITUS LARTIUS, *and other* SENATORS *enter.*

CORIOLANUS
Tullus Aufidius had assembled a new army?

LARTIUS
He had, my lord, and that was why we needed to reach an
agreement sooner than expected.

CORIOLANUS
So then, the Volsces will be able to attack us again when
the time is right.

COMINIUS
They're worn out, lord consul, so we won't likely see
their banners wave again in our lifetime.

CORIOLANUS
Did you see Aufidius?

LARTIUS
He came to me, under tight security, and cursed the
Volsces because they had failed so miserably by letting
the town be captured. He has retreated to Antium.

CORIOLANUS
Did he talk about me?

LARTIUS
He did, my lord.

CORIOLANUS
What did he say?

LARTIUS
He spoke of how often you and he had met in battle. He
said that of all things on earth, he hated you the most and

Your person most, that he would pawn his fortunes
To hopeless restitution, so he might
Be call'd your vanquisher.

CORIOLANUS

                       At Antium lives he?

LARTIUS

5   At Antium.

CORIOLANUS

I wish I had a cause to seek him there,
To oppose his hatred fully. Welcome home.

Enter SICINIUS *and* BRUTUS

Behold, these are the tribunes of the people,
The tongues o' the common mouth: I do despise them;
10   For they do prank them in authority,
Against all noble sufferance.

SICINIUS

Pass no further.

CORIOLANUS

Ha! what is that?

BRUTUS

It will be dangerous to go on: no further.

CORIOLANUS

15   What makes this change?

MENENIUS

The matter?

COMINIUS

Hath he not pass'd the noble and the common?

BRUTUS

Cominius, no.

CORIOLANUS

                     Have I had children's voices?

FIRST SENATOR

20   Tribunes, give way; he shall to the market-place.

that he would pawn his fortunes until he was hopelessly broke in order to defeat you.

CORIOLANUS

He's living in Antium?

LARTIUS

In Antium.

CORIOLANUS

I wish I had a reason to go there and show him how much I hate him, too. Welcome home.

SICINIUS *and* BRUTUS *enter.*

Look, here are the tribunes. I hate them because their authority is an insult to the power of the nobility.

SICINIUS

Go no further.

CORIOLANUS

Ha! What did you say?

BRUTUS

It will be dangerous for you to go any further.

CORIOLANUS

What's changed?

MENENIUS

What's the matter?

COMINIUS

Hasn't he been approved by the nobility and the common people?

BRUTUS

No, Cominius.

CORIOLANUS

Have they broken their promise like children?

FIRST SENATOR

Tribunes, let us through. He's going to the marketplace.

BRUTUS
>The people are incensed against him.

SICINIUS
>   Stop,
>Or all will fall in broil.

CORIOLANUS
>   Are these your herd?
25 Must these have voices, that can yield them now
>And straight disclaim their tongues? What are
>   your offices?
>You being their mouths, why rule you not their teeth?
>Have you not set them on?

MENENIUS
30   Be calm, be calm.

CORIOLANUS
>It is a purposed thing, and grows by plot,
>To curb the will of the nobility:
>Suffer't, and live with such as cannot rule
>Nor ever will be ruled.

BRUTUS
35   Call't not a plot:
>The people cry you mock'd them, and of late,
>When corn was given them gratis, you repined;
>Scandal'd the suppliants for the people, call'd them
>Time-pleasers, flatterers, foes to nobleness.

CORIOLANUS
40 Why, this was known before.

BRUTUS
>   Not to them all.

CORIOLANUS
>Have you inform'd them sithence?

BRUTUS
>   How? I inform them?

CORIOLANUS
>You are like to do such business.

BRUTUS

> The people are furious with him.

SICINIUS

> Stop, or a riot will break out.

CORIOLANUS

> Are these your followers? Why do these people have
> the right to vote, if they can vote one way and then
> immediately change their mind? What's your job? If you
> control what they think and say, can't you control what
> they do? Have you incited them against us?

MENENIUS

> Calm down, calm down.

CORIOLANUS

> It's a deliberate plot to undercut the authority of the
> nobility. If we succumb to it, we'll have to live alongside
> these uncontrollable people who themselves are incapable
> of governing.

BRUTUS

> Don't call it a plot. The people say you mocked them,
> and recently when corn was given to them for free, you
> complained and slandered us, the representatives of the
> people, calling us opportunists, flatterers, and enemies
> to nobility.

CORIOLANUS

> You were already known as such.

BRUTUS

> Not all of them thought so.

CORIOLANUS

> Have you informed them since?

BRUTUS

> How would I inform them?

CORIOLANUS

> By the way you do business.

BRUTUS

45   Not unlike, each way, to better yours.

CORIOLANUS

Why then should I be consul? By yond clouds,
Let me deserve so ill as you, and make me
Your fellow tribune.

SICINIUS

You show too much of that
50   For which the people stir: if you will pass
To where you are bound, you must inquire your way,
Which you are out of, with a gentler spirit,
Or never be so noble as a consul,
Nor yoke with him for tribune.

MENENIUS

55   Let's be calm.

COMINIUS

The people are abused; set on. This paltering
Becomes not Rome, nor has Coriolanus
Deserved this so dishonour'd rub, laid falsely
I' the plain way of his merit.

CORIOLANUS

60   Tell me of corn!
This was my speech, and I will speak't again—

MENENIUS

Not now, not now.

FIRST SENATOR

Not in this heat, sir, now.

CORIOLANUS

Now, as I live, I will. My nobler friends,
65   I crave their pardons:
For the mutable, rank-scented meiny, let them
Regard me as I do not flatter, and
Therein behold themselves: I say again,
In soothing them, we nourish 'gainst our senate
70   The cockle of rebellion, insolence, sedition,

BRUTUS

Possibly, but whatever I do, I do it better than you would do as consul.

CORIOLANUS

Why then should I be consul? If I am as bad as you, make me your fellow tribune.

SICINIUS

You cause too much disturbance among the people. If you want to get where you want to go, you must ask kindly to get there. You're a long way off from doing that. And without doing so, you'll never be noble enough to be consul or even be his equal as a tribune.

MENENIUS

Let's stay calm.

COMINIUS

The people have been deceived and now incited. Trickery like this is not how Romans behave. Coriolanus shouldn't be dishonored by these false accusations because his bravery makes him so clearly deserving.

CORIOLANUS

Talk to me about corn! This was my speech, and I will give it again—

MENENIUS

Not now, not now.

FIRST SENATOR

Not when the people are so agitated, sir, not now.

CORIOLANUS

As sure as I'm alive, I will speak now. My nobler friends, I beg your pardon. As for the two-faced, stinking masses, let them see themselves clearly because I will not flatter them. I say again, by flattering them, we encourage the seeds of rebellion, disobedience, treason against our

Which we ourselves have plough'd for, sow'd, and scatter'd,
By mingling them with us, the honour'd number,
Who lack not virtue, no, nor power, but that
Which they have given to beggars.

MENENIUS

75   Well, no more.

FIRST SENATOR

No more words, we beseech you.

CORIOLANUS

How? No more?
As for my country I have shed my blood,
Not fearing outward force, so shall my lungs
80   Coin words till their decay against those measles,
Which we disdain should tetter us, yet sought
The very way to catch them.

BRUTUS

You speak o' the people,
As if you were a god to punish, not
85   A man of their infirmity.

SICINIUS

'Twere well
We let the people know 't.

MENENIUS

What, what? his choler?

CORIOLANUS

Choler?
90   Were I as patient as the midnight sleep,
By Jove, 'twould be my mind!

SICINIUS

It is a mind
That shall remain a poison where it is,
Not poison any further.

CORIOLANUS

95   "Shall remain"?
Hear you this Triton of the minnows? mark you
His absolute "shall"?

Senate—seeds that we ourselves have plowed for, sowed, and scattered by mingling them with us, the honorable ones. The only virtue or power that we lack is that which we have given to these beggars.

MENENIUS
That's enough, no more.

FIRST SENATOR
No more words, we beg you.

CORIOLANUS
What? No more? I have shed my blood for my country without fearing opposing forces, so my lungs will speak until the hated measles—that we caught by trying to help the people—cause us to become infected and die.

BRUTUS
You speak of the people as if you were a god to punish them, not a mortal man just like them.

SICINIUS
It would be a good idea for us to let the people know this.

MENENIUS
Know what? About his anger?

CORIOLANUS
Anger! If I were as calm as in midnight sleep, by Jove, this would still be my opinion!

SICINIUS
It's a poisonous opinion that shall remain where it is and not poison any further.

CORIOLANUS
"Shall remain"? Do you hear this Triton of the minnows? Do you hear his absolute "shall"?

COMINIUS

'Twas from the canon.

CORIOLANUS

"Shall"?

100   O good but most unwise patricians, why,
       You grave but reckless senators, have you thus
       Given Hydra here to choose an officer,
       That with his peremptory "shall," being but
       The horn and noise o' the monster's, wants not spirit

105   To say he'll turn your current in a ditch,
       And make your channel his? If he have power
       Then vail your ignorance; if none, awake
       Your dangerous lenity. If you are learn'd,
       Be not as common fools; if you are not,

110   Let them have cushions by you. You are plebeians,
       If they be senators: and they are no less,
       When, both your voices blended, the great'st taste
       Most palates theirs. They choose their magistrate,
       And such a one as he, who puts his "shall,"

115   His popular "shall" against a graver bench
       Than ever frown in Greece. By Jove himself!
       It makes the consuls base: and my soul aches
       To know, when two authorities are up,
       Neither supreme, how soon confusion

120   May enter 'twixt the gap of both and take
       The one by the other.

COMINIUS

Well, on to the market-place.

CORIOLANUS

Whoever gave that counsel, to give forth
The corn o' the storehouse gratis, as 'twas used

125   Sometime in Greece,—

MENENIUS

Well, well, no more of that.

COMINIUS

It was inappropriate.

CORIOLANUS

"Shall"! Oh, good but most unwise nobleman! You dignified but reckless senators, why have you permitted this many-headed monster to choose a representative whose arrogant "shall" is just the monster's noisy horn and who has the nerve to say he'll take advantage of your power and use your resources for his own purposes? If he's in power, then it's your mistake that has you bowing to him. If not, then wake up from your dangerous tolerance of him. If you're good leaders, don't be common fools. If you're not, let them have seats with you in the Senate. If they were senators, that would make you into commoners. And if you had equal say, the interests of the common people would outweigh yours. The people chose as their representative someone who addresses his "shall," his common man's command of "shall" to the most dignified legislature since the Greeks. By Jove himself! It lowers the position of the consuls and my soul aches to know, when there are two authorities and neither is supreme, how quickly chaos will arise in the space between them and use one to overthrow the other.

COMINIUS

Let's go on to the marketplace.

CORIOLANUS

Whoever gave the advice to give out corn from the storehouse for free, as they used to do in Greece—

MENENIUS

That's enough. No more talk of that.

CORIOLANUS

> Though there the people had more absolute power,
> I say, they nourish'd disobedience, fed
> The ruin of the state.

BRUTUS

130   Why, shall the people give
> One that speaks thus their voice?

CORIOLANUS

                                                I'll give my reasons,
> More worthier than their voices. They know the corn
> Was not our recompense, resting well assured
135 That ne'er did service for't: being press'd to the war,
> Even when the navel of the state was touch'd,
> They would not thread the gates. This kind of service
> Did not deserve corn gratis. Being i' the war
> Their mutinies and revolts, wherein they show'd
140 Most valour, spoke not for them: the accusation
> Which they have often made against the senate,
> All cause unborn, could never be the motive
> Of our so frank donation. Well, what then?
> How shall this bosom multitude digest
145 The senate's courtesy? Let deeds express
> What's like to be their words: "we did request it;
> We are the greater poll, and in true fear
> They gave us our demands." Thus we debase
> The nature of our seats and make the rabble
150 Call our cares fears; which will in time
> Break ope the locks o' the senate and bring in
> The crows to peck the eagles.

MENENIUS

                                                Come, enough.

BRUTUS

> Enough, with over-measure.

CORIOLANUS

155   No, take more:
> What may be sworn by, both divine and human,

CORIOLANUS

Even though the people had more absolute power
in Greece, I think whoever gave that advice invited
disobedience and caused the ruin of the state.

BRUTUS

Should the people give up someone who speaks for them?

CORIOLANUS

I'll give my reasons, which are worthier than their
wishes. They know they didn't earn the corn, as they
certainly never did any service for it. Even when they
were drafted to fight the war when the center of the state
was threatened, they wouldn't leave the city gates. This
kind of service doesn't deserve free corn. When they
were in the war, their mutinies and revolts, which were
the only times they showed any courage, didn't speak
well for them. Their frequent accusation that the Senate
was hoarding corn had no basis, so it could never be the
reason for our generous gift. Well, what then? How will
this many-headed monster repay the Senate's kindness?
Let their actions express what their words should be:
"We asked for it, we are the majority of the population,
and out of fear they gave in to our demands." In doing
this we degrade the nature of our position and make the
rabble think that our sympathy is fear. In time this will
break open the locks of the Senate, and the scavengers
will devour us.

MENENIUS

Okay, that's enough.

BRUTUS

Enough overstatement.

CORIOLANUS

No, there's more! I swear there's both divine and
human confirmation of what I have to say. A divided

Seal what I end withal! This double worship,
Where one part does disdain with cause, the other
Insult without all reason, where gentry, title, wisdom,
160 Cannot conclude but by the yea and no
Of general ignorance,—it must omit
Real necessities, and give way the while
To unstable slightness: purpose so barr'd, it follows,
Nothing is done to purpose. Therefore, beseech you,—
165 You that will be less fearful than discreet,
That love the fundamental part of state
More than you doubt the change on't, that prefer
A noble life before a long, and wish
To jump a body with a dangerous physic
170 That's sure of death without it, at once pluck out
The multitudinous tongue; let them not lick
The sweet which is their poison: your dishonour
Mangles true judgment and bereaves the state
Of that integrity which should become 't,
175 Not having the power to do the good it would,
For the ill which doth control 't.

BRUTUS

                                                'Has said enough.

SICINIUS

'Has spoken like a traitor, and shall answer
As traitors do.

CORIOLANUS

180   Thou wretch, despite o'erwhelm thee!
What should the people do with these bald tribunes?
On whom depending, their obedience fails
To the greater bench: in a rebellion,
When what's not meet but what must be was law,
185 Then were they chosen: in a better hour,
Let what is meet be said it must be meet,
And throw their power i' the dust.

BRUTUS

Manifest treason!

government—in which one part rightfully despises the
other and the other part makes insulting accusations
without any reason, and in which people of class, title,
and wisdom are reduced to deciding things just by
voting yes or no—will be unable to focus on important
matters and so instead will deal only with trivial
concerns. When governing becomes so difficult, it
makes sense that nothing will get done well. So I beg
you, you who won't be afraid to take action because
you care more about preserving our government
than you fear the consequences of doing so, you who
prefer a noble life over a long one and are willing to
use a dangerous medicine to help someone who would
otherwise surely die, you must immediately remove
the representatives of the common people. Don't let
the tribunes use their poisonous flattery. When they
dishonor you, it's an impediment to justice. It robs the
state of your much-needed integrity and leaves the state
without the power to do the good it would because evil
forces are controlling it.

BRUTUS

He has said enough.

SICINIUS

He has spoken like a traitor and must be punished as
a traitor.

CORIOLANUS

You wretch. I feel overwhelming contempt for you!
Why should the people have these stupid tribunes? By
depending on you, they fail to obey the Senate's higher
authority. In a rebellion, actions that are wrong but
unavoidable are sanctioned because of the circumstances
under which they are chosen. But when times are better,
it must be said that what is right must be done. So throw
the tribunes' power in the garbage.

BRUTUS

That's blatantly treason!

SICINIUS
    This a consul? no.
BRUTUS
190   The aediles, ho!

    Enter an AEDILE.

    Let him be apprehended.
SICINIUS
    Go, call the people.

                        Exit AEDILE.

    (*to* CORIOLANUS) in whose name myself
    Attach thee as a traitorous innovator,
195   A foe to the public weal: obey, I charge thee,
    And follow to thine answer.

                  SICINIUS *tries to seize* CORIOLANUS.
CORIOLANUS
                Hence, old goat!
ALL NOBLES
    We'll surety him.
COMINIUS
          Aged sir, hands off.
CORIOLANUS
200   Hence, rotten thing! or I shall shake thy bones
    Out of thy garments.
SICINIUS
             Help, ye citizens!
    Enter a rabble of CITIZENS, *with the* AEDILES

MENENIUS
    On both sides more respect.
SICINIUS
    Here's he that would take from you all your power.
BRUTUS
205   Seize him, Aediles!

SICINIUS

This man is consul? No.

BRUTUS

An **Aedile**, come here!

A tribune's
assistant

An AEDILE *enters.*

Seize him.

SICINIUS

Go, call the people.

The AEDILE *exits.*

(to CORIOLANUS*)* In the people's name I call you a
traitorous rebel, an enemy of the people. Obey, I
command you, and follow me to your interrogation.

SICINIUS *tries to seize* CORIOLANUS.

CORIOLANUS

Get off me, old goat!

ALL NOBLES

We stand behind him.

COMINIUS

Old man, take your hands off him.

CORIOLANUS

Get off me, you rotten thing! Or I'll shake your bones out
of your clothes.

SICINIUS

Help, you citizens!

A rowdy gang of CITIZENS *enter, with the* AEDILES.

MENENIUS

Both of you, show more respect.

SICINIUS

Here's the man who would take all your power away
from you.

BRUTUS

Seize him, Aediles!

CITIZENS

Down with him! down with him!

ALL NOBLES

Weapons, weapons, weapons!

They all bustle about CORIOLANUS.

Tribunes! Patricians! Citizens! What, ho!

Sicinius! Brutus! Coriolanus! Citizens!

210 "Peace, peace, peace!" "Stay, hold, peace!"

MENENIUS

What is about to be? I am out of breath;

Confusion's near; I cannot speak. You, tribunes

To the people! Coriolanus, patience!

Speak, good Sicinius.

SICINIUS

215   Hear me, people; peace!

CITIZENS

Let's hear our tribune: peace! Speak, speak, speak.

SICINIUS

You are at point to lose your liberties:

Martius would have all from you; Martius,

Whom late you have named for consul.

MENENIUS

220   Fie, fie, fie!

This is the way to kindle, not to quench.

FIRST SENATOR

To unbuild the city and to lay all flat.

SICINIUS

What is the city but the people?

CITIZENS

                                    True,

225 The people are the city.

BRUTUS

By the consent of all, we were establish'd

The people's magistrates.

CITIZENS

You so remain.

CITIZENS

Down with him! Down with him!

ALL NOBLES

Weapons, weapons, weapons!

They all crowd around CORIOLANUS, *shouting.*

Tribunes! Noblemen! Citizens! What's happening?
Sicinius! Brutus! Coriolanus! Citizens! Peace, peace,
peace! Stay, wait, peace!

MENENIUS

What's going to happen? I'm out of breath. Chaos is near.
I can't speak. You tribunes, talk to the people! Coriolanus,
be patient! Speak, good Sicinius.

SICINIUS

Hear me, people. Be calm!

CITIZENS

Let's hear our tribune. Please speak, speak, speak.

SICINIUS

You're about to lose your freedom. Martius will take
everything from you. Martius, who you have just selected
for consul.

MENENIUS

No, no, no! That's the way to incite them further, not
calm them down.

FIRST SENATOR

To destroy the city and tear all the buildings down.

SICINIUS

What is the city if not the people?

CITIZENS

True, the people make the city.

BRUTUS

By everyone's agreement, we were selected to speak for
the people.

CITIZENS

You still do.

MENENIUS

    And so are like to do.

COMINIUS

230   That is the way to lay the city flat;
    To bring the roof to the foundation,
    And bury all, which yet distinctly ranges,
    In heaps and piles of ruin.

SICINIUS

                    This deserves death.

BRUTUS

235   Or let us stand to our authority,
    Or let us lose it. We do here pronounce,
    Upon the part o' the people, in whose power
    We were elected theirs, Martius is worthy
    Of present death.

SICINIUS

240   Therefore lay hold of him;
    Bear him to the rock Tarpeian, and from thence
    Into destruction cast him.

BRUTUS

                  Aediles, seize him!

CITIZENS

    Yield, Martius, yield!

MENENIUS

245   Hear me one word;
    Beseech you, tribunes, hear me but a word.

AEDILE

    Peace, peace!

MENENIUS

    (To BRUTUS*)* Be that you seem, truly your country's friend,
    And temperately proceed to what you would
250   Thus violently redress.

BRUTUS

               Sir, those cold ways,
    That seem like prudent helps, are very poisonous
    Where the disease is violent. Lay hands upon him,

MENENIUS

> And most likely, you're about to speak.

COMINIUS

> That's the way to destroy the city, to bring the roof to the foundation and bury it all, and yet the heaps and piles of ruin have a distinct hierarchy.

SICINIUS

> This deserves death.

BRUTUS

> Either let us exercise our authority, or let us lose it. On behalf of the people who we were elected to represent, we declare that Martius deserves to die immediately.

SICINIUS

> So grab him, take him to the Tarpeian rock, and throw him off the edge.

BRUTUS

> Aediles, seize him!

CITIZENS

> Surrender, Martius, surrender!

MENENIUS

> Let me say one thing. Please, tribunes, let me say just one thing.

AEDILE

> Peace, peace!

MENENIUS

> *(to Brutus)* Act as you should if you're a true servant of your country. Proceed moderately, not with the violent solution you have in mind.

BRUTUS

> Sir, those moderate ways that seem prudent are actually poisonous when the problem is serious. Grab him and take him to the rock.

And bear him to the rock.

CORIOLANUS

255   No, I'll die here.

Drawing his sword

There's some among you have beheld me fighting:
Come, try upon yourselves what you have seen me.

MENENIUS

Down with that sword! Tribunes, withdraw awhile.

BRUTUS

Lay hands upon him.

COMINIUS

260   Help Martius, help,
You that be noble; help him, young and old!

CITIZENS

Down with him, down with him!

In this mutiny, the TRIBUNES, *the* AEDILES,
and the People, are beat in

MENENIUS

(*to* CORIOLANUS) Go, get you to your house; be gone, away!
All will be naught else.

SECOND SENATOR

265   (*to* CORIOLANUS)   Get you gone.

COMINIUS

Stand fast;

We have as many friends as enemies.

MENENIUS

Shall it be put to that?

FIRST SENATOR

(*to* CORIOLANUS)   The gods forbid!

270   I prithee, noble friend, home to thy house;
Leave us to cure this cause.

MENENIUS

For 'tis a sore upon us,

You cannot tent yourself: be gone, beseech you.

COMINIUS

Come, sir, along with us.

CORIOLANUS

No, I'll die here.

He draws his sword.

There's some among you who have seen me fight. Come, try for yourselves to do what you've seen me do in battle.

MENENIUS

Put that sword down! Tribunes, go away for a while.

BRUTUS

Grab him.

COMINIUS

Help Martius, help him, you who are noble. Help him, whether you're young or old!

CITIZENS

Down with him, down with him!

In this mutiny, the **TRIBUNES**, *the* **AEDILES**,
and the people, are forced offstage.

MENENIUS

(to **CORIOLANUS***)* Go home, be gone, go away! All will be lost otherwise.

SECOND SENATOR

(to **CORIOLANUS***)* Get out of here.

COMINIUS

Stay where you are. We have as many allies as enemies.

MENENIUS

Will it come to that?

FIRST SENATOR

(to **CORIOLANUS***)* The gods forbid! I beg you, noble friend, go home. Leave us to handle this situation.

MENENIUS

It's dangerous for all of us now, and you can't fix it yourself. Go now, I beg you.

COMINIUS

Please, sir, come with us.

CORIOLANUS

275   I would they were barbarians—as they are,
Though in Rome litter'd—not Romans—as they are not,
Though calved i' the porch o' the Capitol—

MENENIUS

                                    Be gone;
Put not your worthy rage into your tongue;
280   One time will owe another.

CORIOLANUS

                        On fair ground
I could beat forty of them.

COMINIUS

                       I could myself
Take up a brace o' the best of them; yea, the two tribunes:
285   But now 'tis odds beyond arithmetic;
And manhood is call'd foolery, when it stands
Against a falling fabric. (*to* **CORIOLANUS**) Will you hence,
Before the tag return? whose rage doth rend
Like interrupted waters and o'erbear
290   What they are used to bear.

MENENIUS

(*to* **CORIOLANUS**)   Pray you, be gone:
I'll try whether my old wit be in request
With those that have but little: this must be patch'd
With cloth of any colour.

COMINIUS

295   Nay, come away.

                    Exeunt **CORIOLANUS**, **COMINIUS**, *and others.*

FIRST PATRICIAN

This man has marr'd his fortune.

MENENIUS

His nature is too noble for the world:
He would not flatter Neptune for his trident,
Or Jove for's power to thunder. His heart's his mouth:

CORIOLANUS

I wish they were barbarians—which they are, even though they were born in Rome—and not Romans—which they aren't, even though they were born on the steps of the capitol—

MENENIUS

Go away. You're understandably angry, but stop speaking your anger. There will be time for that in the future.

CORIOLANUS

I could easily beat a large number of them.

COMINIUS

I myself could fight a pair of the best of them—indeed, the two tribunes! But now the odds are beyond calculation, and courage becomes foolishness when it stands beneath a falling building. *(to* CORIOLANUS*)* Will you go now, before the mob returns? Their rage is like dammed up water that will overflow its banks.

MENENIUS

(to CORIOLANUS*)* Please, go now. I'll try to reason with them, even though they're unreasonable. We must try every possible solution to fix this problem.

COMINIUS

Let's go.

CORIOLANUS, COMINIUS, *and others exit.*

FIRST NOBLEMAN

He has ruined himself.

MENENIUS

His nature is too noble for the world. He wouldn't flatter Neptune for his trident or Jove for his power to make thunder. He speaks his mind, and whatever he feels, he

300   What his breast forges, that his tongue must vent;
     And, being angry, does forget that ever
     He heard the name of death.

A noise within.

     Here's goodly work!

SECOND PATRICIAN
     I would they were abed!

MENENIUS
305   I would they were in Tiber! What the vengeance!
     Could he not speak 'em fair?

Re-enter BRUTUS *and* SICINIUS, *with the rabble.*

SICINIUS
                        Where is this viper
     That would depopulate the city and
     Be every man himself?

MENENIUS
310   You worthy tribunes,—

SICINIUS
     He shall be thrown down the Tarpeian rock
     With rigorous hands: he hath resisted law,
     And therefore law shall scorn him further trial
     Than the severity of the public power
315   Which he so sets at nought.

FIRST CITIZEN
                  He shall well know
     The noble tribunes are the people's mouths,
     And we their hands.

CITIZENS
     He shall, sure on't.

MENENIUS
320   Sir, sir—

SICINIUS
     Peace!

must express. And when he gets angry, he forgets that he can also be killed.

A noise comes from offstage.

That was fast!

SECOND NOBLEMAN

I wish they'd gotten away!

MENENIUS

I wish they were in Tiber! What the hell! Couldn't he talk them out of it?

BRUTUS and SICINIUS reenter, with the rabble.

SICINIUS

Where is this traitor that would drive the people from the city and considers himself to be every man?

MENENIUS

You worthy tribunes—

SICINIUS

He'll be thrown without mercy from the Tarpeian rock. He has resisted justice, so justice will deny him any trial other than the strength of public opinion, which to him is worthless.

FIRST CITIZEN

He'll soon know that the noble tribunes speak for the people, and we, in turn, put their wishes into action.

CITIZENS

He will, I'm sure of it.

MENENIUS

Sir, sir—

SICINIUS

Peace!

MENENIUS

Do not cry havoc, where you should but hunt
With modest warrant.

SICINIUS

Sir, how comes't that you
325   Have holp to make this rescue?

MENENIUS

Hear me speak:
As I do know the consul's worthiness,
So can I name his faults—

SICINIUS

Consul! what consul?

MENENIUS

330   The consul Coriolanus.

BRUTUS

He consul!

CITIZENS

No, no, no, no, no.

MENENIUS

If, by the tribunes' leave, and yours, good people,
I may be heard, I would crave a word or two;
335   The which shall turn you to no further harm
Than so much loss of time.

SICINIUS

Speak briefly then;
For we are peremptory to dispatch
This viperous traitor: to eject him hence
340   Were but one danger, and to keep him here
Our certain death: therefore it is decreed
He dies to-night.

MENENIUS

Now the good gods forbid
That our renowned Rome, whose gratitude
345   Towards her deserved children is enroll'd
In Jove's own book, like an unnatural dam
Should now eat up her own!

MENENIUS

> Don't call for his murder. Seek a lesser
> punishment instead.

SICINIUS

> Sir, didn't you help him escape?

MENENIUS

> Listen to me. Because I know this consul's strengths, I
> can also tell you his weaknesses—

SICINIUS

> Consul! What consul?

MENENIUS

> The consul Coriolanus.

BRUTUS

> He's not consul!

CITIZENS

> No, no, no, no, no.

MENENIUS

> Good people, if you and the tribunes will permit me to
> be heard, I want to say a word or two that will cost you
> nothing other than the time it takes to listen.

SICINIUS

> Speak quickly then, for we've agreed to do away with this
> monstrous traitor. To banish him would still leave us in
> danger, and to keep him here would mean our certain
> death, so he must die tonight.

MENENIUS

> The good gods forbid that our renowned Rome, whose
> gratitude toward her deserving children is Jove's law,
> should behave like an unnatural mother and eat her
> own child!

SICINIUS
　　He's a disease that must be cut away.

MENENIUS
　　O, he's a limb that has but a disease;
350　　Mortal, to cut it off; to cure it, easy.
　　What has he done to Rome that's worthy death?
　　Killing our enemies, the blood he hath lost—
　　Which, I dare vouch, is more than that he hath,
　　By many an ounce—he dropp'd it for his country;
355　　And what is left, to lose it by his country,
　　Were to us all, that do't and suffer it,
　　A brand to the end o' the world.

SICINIUS
　　　　　　　　　　　　　　This is clean cam.

BRUTUS
　　Merely awry: when he did love his country,
360　　It honour'd him.

MENENIUS
　　　　　　　　　The service of the foot
　　Being once gangrened, is not then respected
　　For what before it was.

BRUTUS
　　　　　　　　　　We'll hear no more.
365　　Pursue him to his house, and pluck him thence:
　　Lest his infection, being of catching nature,
　　Spread further.

MENENIUS
　　One word more, one word.
　　This tiger-footed rage, when it shall find
370　　The harm of unscann'd swiftness, will too late
　　Tie leaden pounds to's heels. Proceed by process;
　　Lest parties, as he is beloved, break out,
　　And sack great Rome with Romans.

BRUTUS
　　　　　　　　　　　　　　If it were so—

SICINIUS

He's a disease that must be cut out.

MENENIUS

No, he's just a limb that has a disease. It would be fatal to cut off the limb but easy to cure the disease. What has he done to Rome that's worth killing him for? He's killed our enemies and lost more ounces of his own blood than his body still has. He shed it for his country. For his country to take from him the blood he has left would bring eternal shame to all of us who permit it.

SICINIUS

That's totally wrong.

BRUTUS

That's missing the point. When he served his country, it rewarded him.

MENENIUS

When a foot becomes infected with gangrene, is it no longer respected for the service it had done previously?

BRUTUS

We'll hear no more. Go take him from his house, before his contagious infection spreads any further.

MENENIUS

One word more, one word. When this fast-moving rage realizes the consequences of acting quickly without thinking, it will be too late to slow it down. Let the legal system solve this dispute, otherwise factions will form, as there are those who support him, and Rome will be destroyed by Romans.

BRUTUS

If that were true—

SICINIUS

375   What do ye talk?
        Have we not had a taste of his obedience?
        Our aediles smote? Ourselves resisted? Come.

MENENIUS

        Consider this: he has been bred i' the wars
        Since he could draw a sword, and is ill school'd
380   In bolted language; meal and bran together
        He throws without distinction. Give me leave,
        I'll go to him, and undertake to bring him
        Where he shall answer, by a lawful form,
        In peace, to his utmost peril.

FIRST SENATOR

385   Noble tribunes,
        It is the humane way: the other course
        Will prove too bloody, and the end of it
        Unknown to the beginning.

SICINIUS

                          Noble Menenius,
390   Be you then as the people's officer.
        Masters, lay down your weapons.

BRUTUS

                              Go not home.

SICINIUS

        Meet on the market-place. We'll attend you there:
        Where, if you bring not Martius, we'll proceed
395   In our first way.

MENENIUS

        I'll bring him to you.
        (*to the* SENATORS) Let me desire your company: he
                must come,
        Or what is worst will follow.

FIRST SENATOR

                          Pray you, let's to him.
400

                                      Exeunt.

SICINIUS

What are you talking about? Haven't we experienced his obedience? Haven't our aediles been struck by him? Haven't our own efforts been resisted? Come.

MENENIUS

Consider that he's been brought up in wars since he was old enough to draw a sword. He doesn't know how to use refined language. He can't tell the difference between meal and bran. Let me go to him and try to convince him to answer your questions peacefully in court. Legal judgment may still cost him his life.

FIRST SENATOR

Noble tribunes, this is the humane way. The other course of action will prove too bloody, and we have no idea what we're getting ourselves into.

SICINIUS

Noble Menenius, you may act on behalf of the people. Good people, lay your weapons down.

BRUTUS

Don't go home.

SICINIUS

Meet us in the marketplace. We'll wait for you there. If you don't bring Martius, we'll continue with our original plans.

MENENIUS

I'll bring him to you.
(to the Senators) Come with me. We must bring him, or something worse will happen.

FIRST SENATOR

Yes, let's go to him.

All exit.

ACT 3, SCENE 2

A room in Coriolanus's house.
Enter CORIOLANUS *with Patricians.*

CORIOLANUS
Let them pull all about mine ears, present me
Death on the wheel or at wild horses' heels,
Or pile ten hills on the Tarpeian rock,
That the precipitation might down stretch
5   Below the beam of sight, yet will I still
Be thus to them.

A PATRICIAN
You do the nobler.

CORIOLANUS
I muse my mother
Does not approve me further, who was wont
10   To call them woollen vassals, things created
To buy and sell with groats, to show bare heads
In congregations, to yawn, be still and wonder,
When one but of my ordinance stood up
To speak of peace or war.

Enter VOLUMNIA

15   I talk of you:
Why did you wish me milder? would you have me
False to my nature? Rather say I play
The man I am.

VOLUMNIA
                                   O, sir, sir, sir,
20   I would have had you put your power well on,
Before you had worn it out.

CORIOLANUS
Let go.

ACT 3, SCENE 2

A room in Coriolanus's house.
CORIOLANUS *enters with Noblemen.*

CORIOLANUS
Let them shout their fury. They can put me to death on
the wheel, let wild horses drag me, or pile ten hills on the
Tarpeian rock, making the fall so far that you can't see the
bottom. It won't change who I am compared to them.

A NOBLEMAN
You are nobler than they are.

CORIOLANUS
I wonder if my mother still sides with me. She used to call
them slaves in rough wool clothes, traders of cheap items
who were always taking their hats off to those of higher
rank and whose jaws dropped in silent amazement when
someone like me made speeches about peace or war.

VOLUMNIA *enters.*

I'm talking about you. Why did you want me to be more
subdued? Would you have me be untrue to my nature?
Would you rather I pretend to be someone else?

VOLUMNIA
Oh, sir, sir, sir, I wanted your power to be made official
before you used it up.

CORIOLANUS
Stop it.

VOLUMNIA
> You might have been enough the man you are,
> With striving less to be so; lesser had been
25 The thwartings of your dispositions, if
> You had not show'd them how ye were disposed
> Ere they lack'd power to cross you.

CORIOLANUS
>   Let them hang!

VOLUMNIA
> Ay, and burn too.

Enter MENENIUS *and* SENATORS

MENENIUS
30 (to CORIOLANUS) Come, come, you have been too rough,
>   something too rough;
> You must return and mend it.

FIRST SENATOR
>   There's no remedy;
> Unless, by not so doing, our good city
35 Cleave in the midst and perish.

VOLUMNIA
>   Pray, be counsell'd:
> I have a heart as little apt as yours,
> But yet a brain that leads my use of anger
> To better vantage.

MENENIUS
40   Well said, noble woman!
> Before he should thus stoop to the herd, but that
> The violent fit o' the time craves it as physic
> For the whole state, I would put mine armour on,
> Which I can scarcely bear.

CORIOLANUS
>   What must I do?
45

MENENIUS
> Return to the tribunes.

VOLUMNIA

You would've been enough of a man without fighting so hard to prove yourself. The people wouldn't have condemned you if you hadn't shown them your true disposition before they lost the power to stop you.

CORIOLANUS

Let them hang.

VOLUMNIA

Yes, and burn, too.

MENENIUS *and* SENATORS *enter.*

MENENIUS

(*to* CORIOLANUS) Come, come, you've been a bit too rough. You must go back and fix things with the people.

FIRST SENATOR

There's no remedy. Unless you go, our good city will break in two and be ruined.

VOLUMNIA

Please, listen to this advice. I'm as stubborn as you are, but I'm smart enough to use my anger to my advantage.

MENENIUS

Well said, noble woman. Before he returns to the masses, given the current violent climate in the state, which demands a solution to this problem, I'd like to put my armor on, even though I am barely strong enough to wear it.

CORIOLANUS

What should I do?

MENENIUS

Return to the tribunes.

CORIOLANUS
                              Well, what then? what then?

MENENIUS
         Repent what you have spoke.

CORIOLANUS
         For them! I cannot do it to the gods;
50   Must I then do 't to them?

VOLUMNIA
                                    You are too absolute;
         Though therein you can never be too noble,
         But when extremities speak. I have heard you say,
         Honour and policy, like unsever'd friends,
55   I' the war do grow together: grant that, and tell me,
         In peace what each of them by the other lose,
         That they combine not there.

CORIOLANUS
                                    Tush, tush!

MENENIUS
                                          A good demand.

VOLUMNIA
60   If it be honour in your wars to seem
         The same you are not, which, for your best ends,
         You adopt your policy, how is it less or worse,
         That it shall hold companionship in peace
         With honour, as in war, since that to both
65   It stands in like request?

CORIOLANUS
                              Why force you this?

VOLUMNIA
         Because that now it lies you on to speak
         To the people; not by your own instruction,
         Nor by the matter which your heart prompts you,
70   But with such words that are but rooted in
         Your tongue, though but bastards and syllables
         Of no allowance to your bosom's truth.
         Now, this no more dishonours you at all

CORIOLANUS

And then what?

MENENIUS

Take back what you said.

CORIOLANUS

For them! I can't take back what I've said to the gods, but must I take back what I've said to the people?

VOLUMNIA

You're too rigid. You can never be too noble, except in extreme circumstances. I've heard you say that in war, honor and strategy go together. If that's the case, tell me, why wouldn't they also go together in times of peace?

CORIOLANUS

Hush, hush!

MENENIUS

That's a good question.

VOLUMNIA

If it's honorable in war to pretend to be other than how you are, if it serves your end goal, why is it less honorable to do so in times of peace?

CORIOLANUS

Why do you ask?

VOLUMNIA

Because you have to speak to the people now—and not to give them instructions or to talk from your heart. What you say can't reflect the truth of what you really feel. However, this doesn't dishonor you any more than it would to capture a town with flattering words, a town that would otherwise take your fortune and spill your blood. I would feel it honorable to hide my real nature if

Than to take in a town with gentle words,
75   Which else would put you to your fortune and
'The hazard of much blood.
I would dissemble with my nature where
My fortunes and my friends at stake required
I should do so in honour: I am in this,
80   Your wife, your son, these senators, the nobles;
And you will rather show our general louts
How you can frown than spend a fawn upon 'em,
For the inheritance of their loves and safeguard
Of what that want might ruin.

MENENIUS
85   Noble lady!
Come, go with us; speak fair: you may salve so,
Not what is dangerous present, but the loss
Of what is past.

VOLUMNIA
                                    I prithee now, my son,
90   Go to them, with this bonnet in thy hand;
And thus far having stretch'd it—here be with them—
Thy knee bussing the stones—for in such business
Action is eloquence, and the eyes of the ignorant
More learned than the ears—waving thy head,
95   Which often, thus, correcting thy stout heart,
Now humble as the ripest mulberry
That will not hold the handling: or say to them,
Thou art their soldier, and being bred in broils
Hast not the soft way which, thou dost confess,
100   Were fit for thee to use as they to claim,
In asking their good loves, but thou wilt frame
Thyself, forsooth, hereafter theirs, so far
As thou hast power and person.

MENENIUS   (*to* CORIOLANUS) This but done,
Even as she speaks, why, their hearts were yours;
105   For they have pardons, being ask'd, as free
As words to little purpose.

my fortune and my friends were at risk. I speak for your wife, your son, these senators, and the nobles about this: you'd prefer to show the miserable commoners how you frown than flatter them in any way, even for the sake of their approval and to protect what might be ruined without it.

MENENIUS

Noble lady! Come with us. Your honest words may heal not only present dangers but also past losses.

VOLUMNIA

I beg you now, my son, go to them, with your hat in your hand. And once you've extended your hat to them—do what they ask—get on your knees and kiss the ground, bow your head and humble your proud heart like the ripest mulberry that falls from the branch the moment it's touched—for in this situation actions speak louder than words. Or tell them that you are their soldier and admit that because you were raised on the battlefield, you never learned a gentle way with words, but you realize you should have spoken more kindly when asking for their votes. Tell them that you'll work for their benefit from here on out, to the extent of your political power and physical ability.

MENENIUS

(To CORIOLANUS*)* Do as she says, and their hearts will belong to you. If you ask, they'll pardon you as easily as they speak their nonsense.

VOLUMNIA
                              Prithee now,
        Go, and be ruled: although I know thou hadst rather
        Follow thine enemy in a fiery gulf
110   Than flatter him in a bower.

        Enter COMINIUS

                                          Here is Cominius.
COMINIUS
        I have been i' the marketplace; and, sir, 'tis fit
        You make strong party, or defend yourself
        By calmness or by absence: all's in anger.
MENENIUS
115   Only fair speech.
COMINIUS
                              I think 'twill serve, if he
        Can thereto frame his spirit.
VOLUMNIA
                                        He must, and will
        Prithee now, say you will, and go about it.
CORIOLANUS
120   Must I go show them my unbarbed sconce?
        Must I with base tongue give to my noble heart
        A lie that it must bear? Well, I will do 't:
        Yet, were there but this single plot to lose,
        This mould of Martius, they to dust should grind it
125   And throw 't against the wind. To the marketplace!
        You have put me now to such a part which never
        I shall discharge to the life.
COMINIUS
                                    Come, come, we'll prompt you.
VOLUMNIA
        I prithee now, sweet son, as thou hast said
130   My praises made thee first a soldier, so,
        To have my praise for this, perform a part
        Thou hast not done before.

VOLUMNIA

Please, go now. Submit to them, although I know you'd
rather pursue your enemy through the fires of hell than
flatter him in a boudoir.

COMINIUS *enters.*

Here's Cominius.

COMINIUS

Sir, I've been in the marketplace. You'll need to argue
your case strongly or defend yourself with calmness—or
don't come at all. Everyone is angry.

MENENIUS

Just speak kindly.

COMINIUS

I think that'll work, if he can control his temper.

VOLUMNIA

He must, and I beg you, say you will and then go do it.

CORIOLANUS

Do I have to show them my head without a helmet?
Do I have to betray my heart and speak words that are
lies? Well, I'll do it. But if I lose, they'll grind me into
dust and throw it against the wind. To the marketplace!
You're asking me to play a part that I will never
play convincingly.

COMINIUS

Come, come, we'll tell you what to say.

VOLUMNIA

I beg you now, sweet son. You've said that my
encouragement is what made you into a soldier, so I
encourage you now to play this new role.

CORIOLANUS

       Well, I must do't:
Away, my disposition, and possess me
135 Some harlot's spirit! my throat of war be turn'd,
Which choired with my drum, into a pipe
Small as a eunuch, or the virgin voice
That babies lull asleep! the smiles of knaves
Tent in my cheeks, and schoolboys' tears take up
140 The glasses of my sight! a beggar's tongue
Make motion through my lips, and my arm'd knees,
Who bow'd but in my stirrup, bend like his
That hath received an alms! I will not do't,
Lest I surcease to honour mine own truth
145 And, by my body's action, teach my mind
A most inherent baseness.

VOLUMNIA

       At thy choice, then:
To beg of thee, it is my more dishonour
Than thou of them. Come all to ruin; let
150 Thy mother rather feel thy pride than fear
Thy dangerous stoutness, for I mock at death
With as big heart as thou. Do as thou list
Thy valiantness was mine, thou suck'st it from me,
But owe thy pride thyself.

CORIOLANUS

155   Pray, be content:
Mother, I am going to the marketplace;
Chide me no more. I'll mountebank their loves,
Cog their hearts from them, and come home beloved
Of all the trades in Rome. Look, I am going:
160 Commend me to my wife. I'll return consul;
Or never trust to what my tongue can do
I' the way of flattery further.

VOLUMNIA

       Do your will.

      VOLUMNIA *Exits.*

CORIOLANUS

Well, I must do it. I'll hide my true nature and become like a whore! My voice, which ordinarily calls for war, will harmonize with my drum and become the voice of a eunuch or a virgin that sings babies to sleep! I'll smile like a servant, cry like a schoolboy, and speak like a beggar! My armored knees, which ordinarily only bend in my saddle, will bend like a man receiving alms! I won't do it because it will dishonor my true nature, and what I do with my body will degrade my mind.

VOLUMNIA

This is your choice then. It is more dishonorable for me to have to beg you than for you to have to beg them. Everything will be ruined. I'd rather endure the consequences of challenging your pride than be afraid of it, for I fear death as little as you do. Do as you please. Your courage comes from me—you sucked it from me as a nursing baby—but your pride is all your own.

CORIOLANUS

That's enough, mother. I'm going to the marketplace. Don't scold me any further. I'll deceive them into liking me, steal their hearts, and come home beloved by all the tradesmen in Rome. Look, I'm going. Give my regards to my wife. I'll come back as consul. Never again doubt how well my tongue can flatter.

VOLUMNIA

Do what you need to do.

VOLUMNIA *exits.*

COMINIUS

    Away! the tribunes do attend you: arm yourself
165   To answer mildly; for they are prepared
    With accusations, as I hear, more strong
    Than are upon you yet.

CORIOLANUS

    The word is "mildly." Pray you, let us go:
    Let them accuse me by invention, I
170   Will answer in mine honour.

MENENIUS

                           Ay, but mildly.

CORIOLANUS

    Well, mildly be it then. Mildly!

                                   Exeunt.

COMINIUS

> Go! The tribunes are waiting for you. Be prepared to answer questions mildly. I've heard that they have even stronger accusations than the ones they've made so far.

CORIOLANUS

> The key word is "mild." Please, let's go. Let them invent accusations against me, and I'll answer honorably.

MENENIUS

> Yes, but mildly.

CORIOLANUS

> Well, mildly it will be then. Mildly!

All exit.

ACT 3, SCENE 3

The Forum.
Enter SICINIUS *and* BRUTUS

BRUTUS
      In this point charge him home, that he affects
      Tyrannical power: if he evade us there,
      Enforce him with his envy to the people,
      And that the spoil got on the Antiates
5   Was ne'er distributed.

      Enter an AEDILE.

      What, will he come?
AEDILE
      He's coming.
BRUTUS
      How accompanied?
AEDILE
      With old Menenius, and those senators
10   That always favour'd him.
SICINIUS
                                    Have you a catalogue
      Of all the voices that we have procured
      Set down by the poll?
AEDILE
                                    I have; 'tis ready.
SICINIUS
15   Have you collected them by tribes?
AEDILE
                                                I have.
SICINIUS
      Assemble presently the people hither;
      And when they hear me say "It shall be so
      I' the right and strength o' the commons," be it either

ACT 3, SCENE 3

The Forum.
SICINIUS *and* BRUTUS *enter.*

BRUTUS

Drive this point home: his aim is to be a tyrant. If he dodges this accusation, confront him with his ill-will toward the people, and that the spoils won from the Antiates were never distributed.

An AEDILE *enters.*

Is he coming?

AEDILE

He's coming.

BRUTUS

Who's he with?

AEDILE

With old Menenius and those senators that have always favored him.

SICINIUS

Do you have a list of all the individual votes taken in our poll?

AEDILE

I do. It's ready.

SICINIUS

Have you counted them by district?

AEDILE

I have.

SICINIUS

Bring the people here now, and when I say, "The decision of the people is," whether it's death, fine, or banishment, if I say, "fine," have them cry, "Fine," if "death,"

20 For death, for fine, or banishment, then let them
If I say fine, cry "Fine"; if death, cry "Death."
Insisting on the old prerogative
And power i' the truth o' the cause.

AEDILE

I shall inform them.

BRUTUS

25 And when such time they have begun to cry,
Let them not cease, but with a din confused
Enforce the present execution
Of what we chance to sentence.

AEDILE

Very well.

SICINIUS

30 Make them be strong and ready for this hint,
When we shall hap to give 't them.

BRUTUS

Go about it.

Exit Aedile.

Put him to choler straight: he hath been used
Ever to conquer, and to have his worth
35 Of contradiction: being once chafed, he cannot
Be rein'd again to temperance; then he speaks
What's in his heart; and that is there which looks
With us to break his neck.

SICINIUS

Well, here he comes.

Enter CORIOLANUS, MENENIUS, *and* COMINIUS, *with Senators and Patricians.*

MENENIUS

40 (*aside to Coriolanus*) Calmly, I do beseech you.

CORIOLANUS

Ay, as an hostler, that for the poorest piece
Will bear the knave by the volume. The honour'd gods

cry, "Death." They must insist on their legal right to decide this and the power that comes from the truth of their cause.

AEDILE

I'll tell them.

BRUTUS

And when they begin to cry out, don't let them stop. The chaotic noise will force their decision to be carried out on the spot.

AEDILE

Very well.

SICINIUS

Prepare them for this. They have to be able to get the signal when we give it to them.

BRUTUS

Do it.

The Aedile exits.

Get him angry right away. He's accustomed to always winning and being as contrary as he pleases. Once he's provoked, he won't be able to rein in his temper. Then he'll say how he really feels, and most likely we can use that as reason to break his neck.

SICINIUS

Well, here he comes.

CORIOLANUS, MENENIUS, *and* COMINIUS *enter, with Senators and Noblemen.*

MENENIUS

(*aside to Coriolanus*) Stay calm, I beg you.

CORIOLANUS

Yes, like a stable boy that for the smallest amount of money will tolerate being called a slave over and over

Keep Rome in safety, and the chairs of justice
Supplied with worthy men! plant love among 's!
45   Throng our large temples with the shows of peace,
And not our streets with war!

FIRST SENATOR
                                                    Amen, amen.

MENENIUS
A noble wish.

Re-enter the Aedile, with the CITIZENS.

SICINIUS
Draw near, you people.

AEDILE
50   List to your tribunes. Audience: peace, I say!

CORIOLANUS
First, hear me speak.

BOTH TRIBUNES
Well, say. Peace, ho!

CORIOLANUS
Shall I be charged no further than this present?
Must all determine here?

SICINIUS
                                        I do demand,
55   If you submit you to the people's voices,
Allow their officers and are content
To suffer lawful censure for such faults
As shall be proved upon you?

CORIOLANUS
                                        I am content.

60

MENENIUS
Lo, citizens, he says he is content:
The warlike service he has done, consider; think
Upon the wounds his body bears, which show
Like graves i' the holy churchyard.

again. May the honored gods protect Rome and supply the chairs of justice with worthy men! Let there be love among us! Fill our large temples with demonstrations of peace and not our streets with war!

FIRST SENATOR

Amen, amen.

MENENIUS

A noble wish.

The Aedile re-enters, with CITIZENS.

SICINIUS

Come close, you people.

AEDILE

Listen to your tribunes. Be quiet!

CORIOLANUS

Let me speak first.

BOTH TRIBUNES

Well then, talk! Stay calm.

CORIOLANUS

Are there any further charges against me besides these? Will everything be settled here?

SICINIUS

Will you agree to listen to the people, respect their representatives, and undergo lawful punishment for the offenses we'll prove you committed?

CORIOLANUS

Yes, I agree.

MENENIUS

All right citizens, he says he agrees. Think of the wars he has served in. Think about the wounds on his body— each of them is like an enemy's gravestone.

CORIOLANUS

65   Scratches with briers,
Scars to move laughter only.

MENENIUS

Consider further,
That when he speaks not like a citizen,
You find him like a soldier: do not take
70   His rougher accents for malicious sounds,
But, as I say, such as become a soldier,
Rather than envy you.

COMINIUS

Well, well, no more.

CORIOLANUS

What is the matter
75   That being pass'd for consul with full voice,
I am so dishonour'd that the very hour
You take it off again?

SICINIUS

Answer to us.

CORIOLANUS

Say, then: 'tis true, I ought so.

SICINIUS

80   We charge you, that you have contrived to take
From Rome all season'd office and to wind
Yourself into a power tyrannical;
For which you are a traitor to the people.

CORIOLANUS

How? Traitor!

MENENIUS

85   Nay, temperately; your promise.

CORIOLANUS

The fires i' the lowest hell fold in the people!
Call me their traitor? Thou injurious tribune!
Within thine eyes sat twenty thousand deaths,
In thy hands clutch'd as many millions, in
90   Thy lying tongue both numbers, I would say

CORIOLANUS

They're no more serious than scratches from a prickly plant. They're scars that you'd only laugh at.

MENENIUS

Consider also that because he doesn't speak like you, you think he's attacking you. Don't mistake his coarse way of speaking for hateful words. He's just talking the way soldiers talk. He's not speaking ill of you.

COMINIUS

Okay, that's enough.

CORIOLANUS

How did it happen that I was approved for consul with a unanimous vote and in the next moment I'm disgraced by a change of opinion?

SICINIUS

Answer our questions.

CORIOLANUS

Well it's true then. I thought so.

SICINIUS

We accuse you of trying to do away with the established legal system in Rome and to put yourself in a position of tyrannical power. For this you are a traitor to the people.

CORIOLANUS

How am I a traitor?

MENENIUS

No, stay calm. You promised.

CORIOLANUS

May the people fall into the fires of the lowest hell! You're calling me a traitor? You slanderous tribune! If your eyes had killed twenty thousand people, your hands had killed a million, and your lying tongue had killed those numbers together, I would still say to you, "You lie" with a voice as

"Thou liest" unto thee with a voice as free
As I do pray the gods.

SICINIUS

Mark you this, people?

CITIZENS

To the rock, to the rock with him!

SICINIUS

95 Peace!
We need not put new matter to his charge:
What you have seen him do and heard him speak,
Beating your officers, cursing yourselves,
Opposing laws with strokes and here defying
100 Those whose great power must try him; even this,
So criminal and in such capital kind,
Deserves the extremest death.

BRUTUS

But since he hath
Served well for Rome,—

CORIOLANUS

105 What do you prate of service?

BRUTUS

I talk of that that know it.

CORIOLANUS

You?

MENENIUS

Is this the promise that you made your mother?

COMINIUS

Know, I pray you—

CORIOLANUS

110 I know no further:
Let them pronounce the steep Tarpeian death,
Vagabond exile, flaying, pent to linger
But with a grain a day, I would not buy
Their mercy at the price of one fair word;
115 Nor cheque my courage for what they can give,
To have't with saying "Good morrow."

honest as the one I pray to the gods with.

SICINIUS

Do you hear this, people?

CITIZENS

Throw him from the rock!

SICINIUS

Peace! We don't need to aggravate him further. What you've seen him do and heard him say—beating your officers, speaking ill of you, opposing our laws with force, and now defying those who have the great power to put him on trial—even this, which is criminal and punishable by death, deserves the most severe penalty.

BRUTUS

But since he has served Rome so well—

CORIOLANUS

Why do you talk about service?

BRUTUS

I talk about what I know.

CORIOLANUS

What do you know about service?

MENENIUS

Is this the promise that you made your mother?

COMINIUS

Listen, I beg you—

CORIOLANUS

I'll listen no more. Let them throw me from the steep Tarpeian rock, make me a wandering exile, skin me alive, or condemn me to live on just a grain a day. I wouldn't buy their mercy at the cost of the truth, nor would I hold back my beliefs for the freedom they can give me, if I had to say to them, "Good day."

SICINIUS

For that he has,
As much as in him lies, from time to time
Envied against the people, seeking means
120   To pluck away their power, as now at last
Given hostile strokes, and that not in the presence
Of dreaded justice, but on the ministers
That do distribute it; in the name o' the people
And in the power of us the tribunes, we,
125   Even from this instant, banish him our city,
In peril of precipitation
From off the rock Tarpeian never more
To enter our Rome gates: i' the people's name,
I say it shall be so.

CITIZENS

130   It shall be so, it shall be so; let him away:
He's banish'd, and it shall be so.

COMINIUS

Hear me, my masters, and my common friends,—

SICINIUS

He's sentenced; no more hearing.

COMINIUS

Let me speak:
135   I have been consul, and can show for Rome
Her enemies' marks upon me. I do love
My country's good with a respect more tender,
More holy and profound, than mine own life,
My dear wife's estimate, her womb's increase,
140   And treasure of my loins; then if I would
Speak that,—

SICINIUS

We know your drift: speak what?

BRUTUS

There's no more to be said, but he is banish'd,
As enemy to the people and his country:
145   It shall be so.

SICINIUS

As much as he could, he has continually conspired
against the people, looking for ways to take away their
power, and now he's finally taken violent measures,
and not only in front of justice itself but also those who
attempt to carry it out. In the name of the people and by
our power as tribunes, from this moment forward we
banish him from our city. If he ever enters the gates of
Rome again, he will be thrown off the Tarpeian rock. I
declare this on behalf of the people.

CITIZENS

It shall be so, it shall be so. Take him away. He's
banished, and it shall be so.

COMINIUS

Listen to me, good people, my friends—

SICINIUS

He's been sentenced. There's nothing more to say.

COMINIUS

Let me speak. I have been consul, and I can show you
the wounds I've received fighting for Rome. My feelings
about the welfare of my country are more tender, more
holy, and more profound than how I feel about my own
life, my dear wife's reputation, her ability to bear my
precious children. So I would like to say—

SICINIUS

We know your loyalty. What do you want to say?

BRUTUS

There's no more to be said: he is banished as enemy of the
people and his country. It shall be so.

CITIZENS
> It shall be so, it shall be so.

CORIOLANUS
> You common cry of curs, whose breath I hate
> As reek o' the rotten fens, whose loves I prize
> As the dead carcasses of unburied men
150 That do corrupt my air, I banish you;
> And here remain with your uncertainty!
> Let every feeble rumour shake your hearts!
> Your enemies, with nodding of their plumes,
> Fan you into despair! Have the power still
155 To banish your defenders; till at length
> Your ignorance, which finds not till it feels,
> Making not reservation of yourselves,
> Still your own foes, deliver you as most
> Abated captives to some nation
160 That won you without blows! Despising,
> For you, the city, thus I turn my back:
> There is a world elsewhere.

> *Exeunt* CORIOLANUS, COMINIUS, MENENIUS,
> *Senators, and Patricians.*

AEDILE
> The people's enemy is gone, is gone!

CITIZENS
> Our enemy is banish'd! he is gone! Hoo! hoo!
> *Shouting, and throwing up their caps.*

SICINIUS
165 Go, see him out at gates, and follow him,
> As he hath followed you, with all despite;
> Give him deserved vexation. Let a guard
> Attend us through the city.

CITIZENS
> Come, come; let's see him out at gates; come.
170 The gods preserve our noble tribunes! Come.
> *Exeunt.*

CITIZENS

It shall be so, it shall be so.

CORIOLANUS

You pack of common dogs! Your breath reeks like the rotting swamps. I value your opinion of me as much as the dead carcasses of unburied men that stink up my air. I banish you! Stay here with your indecisiveness and let every feeble rumor change your minds. When you see your enemies plumed helmets approaching, may you fall into despair! May you retain the power to banish the ones who would protect you, until at last your ignorance— which makes you unable to foresee anything before it happens and leaves you alone in the city as your own worst enemy—leads you to be captured by some nation that defeated you without a fight! With hatred, I turn my back on you and the city. I will seek a new life elsewhere.

CORIOLANUS, COMINIUS, MENENIUS, Senators, and the Noblemen exit.

AEDILE

The people's enemy is gone. He is gone!

CITIZENS

Our enemy is banished! He is gone! Yoo-hoo!

They shout and throw up their caps.

SICINIUS

Go, see him go out the gates, and look at him with contempt, as he looked at you. Torment him—he deserves it. Let a parade follow us through the city.

CITIZENS

Come, come. Let's see him go out the gates. Come. May the gods protect our noble tribunes! Come.

All exit.

ACT FOUR

SCENE 1

Rome. Before a gate of the city.
Enter CORIOLANUS, VOLUMNIA, VIRGILIA, MENENIUS,
COMINIUS, *with the young Nobility of Rome*

CORIOLANUS

Come, leave your tears: a brief farewell: the beast
With many heads butts me away. Nay, mother,
Where is your ancient courage? you were used
To say extremity was the trier of spirits;
That common chances common men could bear;
That when the sea was calm all boats alike
Show'd mastership in floating; fortune's blows,
When most struck home, being gentle wounded, craves
A noble cunning: you were used to load me
With precepts that would make invincible
The heart that conn'd them.

VIRGILIA

O heavens! O heavens!

CORIOLANUS

       Nay! prithee, woman,—

VOLUMNIA

Now the red pestilence strike all trades in Rome,
And occupations perish!

CORIOLANUS

        What, what, what!
I shall be loved when I am lack'd. Nay, mother.
Resume that spirit, when you were wont to say,
If you had been the wife of Hercules,
Six of his labours you'ld have done, and saved
Your husband so much sweat. Cominius,
Droop not; adieu. Farewell, my wife, my mother:
I'll do well yet. Thou old and true Menenius,

ACT FOUR
SCENE 1

A city gate in Rome.
CORIOLANUS, VOLUMNIA, VIRGILIA, MENENIUS, *and*
COMINIUS *enter, with the young nobles.*

CORIOLANUS

Stop crying now. A brief farewell! The people, like a
many-headed beast, push me out. Stop it, mother. What
happened to your courage? You used to say that adversity
was a test of character. That even common people can
handle the chance circumstances of their lives. That when
the sea is calm all boats float equally well. That when fate
strikes you hardest, you must have the skill of a nobleman
to endure your wounds with dignity. You used to repeat
these sayings to me, sayings that would make anyone who
heard them enough invincible.

VIRGILIA

Oh, heavens! Oh, heavens!

CORIOLANUS

Stop it! Please, woman—

VOLUMNIA

Now the typhoid fever strikes all the tradesmen in Rome
and the economy is crumbling!

CORIOLANUS

Enough, enough, enough! You'll love me when I'm gone.
Stop it, mother. Bring back your old spirit, when you
used to say that if you had been the wife of Hercules,
you would have done six of his twelve required tasks and
saved him that much effort. Cominius, don't despair.
Goodbye. Farewell, my wife, my mother—I'll be fine.
My old and true friend Menenius, you cry more than a

Thy tears are salter than a younger man's,
And venomous to thine eyes. My sometime general,
I have seen thee stern, and thou hast oft beheld
Heart-hardening spectacles; tell these sad women
5   'Tis fond to wail inevitable strokes,
As 'tis to laugh at 'em. My mother, you wot well
My hazards still have been your solace: and
Believe't not lightly—though I go alone,
Like to a lonely dragon, that his fen
10   Makes fear'd and talk'd of more than seen—your son
Will or exceed the common or be caught
With cautelous baits and practise.

VOLUMNIA
                                        My first son.
Whither wilt thou go? Take good Cominius
15   With thee awhile: determine on some course,
More than a wild exposture to each chance
That starts i' the way before thee.

CORIOLANUS
                                        O the gods!

COMINIUS
I'll follow thee a month, devise with thee
20   Where thou shalt rest, that thou mayst hear of us
And we of thee: so if the time thrust forth
A cause for thy repeal, we shall not send
O'er the vast world to seek a single man,
And lose advantage, which doth ever cool
25   I' the absence of the needer.

CORIOLANUS
                                        Fare ye well:
Thou hast years upon thee; and thou art too full
Of the wars' surfeits, to go rove with one
That's yet unbruised: bring me but out at gate.
30   Come, my sweet wife, my dearest mother, and
My friends of noble touch, when I am forth,
Bid me farewell, and smile. I pray you, come.

young man, and the salt is bad for your eyes. My former
general, I have seen you be brave, and you have seen
many heart-hardening spectacles. Tell these sad women
that it's as foolish to cry over inevitabilities as it is to
laugh at them. Mother, you've always taken comfort in
the risks that I take. Know this for a fact: even though
I go alone, like a lonely dragon whose swamp is more
feared and talked about than it is seen, I will either
exceed common expectations or be caught by crafty traps
and trickery.

VOLUMNIA

My firstborn son, where will you go? Take good
Cominius with you for a while. Figure out a plan other
than just dealing with things as they come up.

CORIOLANUS

Oh, the gods!

COMINIUS

I'll go with you for a month and help you find a place to
stay and a way to communicate with us. That way, if they
overturn your sentence, we won't have to look all over the
world to find you and lose momentum on your return.

CORIOLANUS

No, I must go alone. You're too old, and you've been in
too many wars to go roaming around with someone like
me, who's still fresh. Just take me to the gate. Come, my
sweet wife, my dearest mother, and my noble friends.
When I go, wish me safe travels and smile. I promise
that so long as I'm still alive you'll hear from me, and the
news will be the same as it's always been about me.

While I remain above the ground, you shall
Hear from me still, and never of me aught
35   But what is like me formerly.

MENENIUS

That's worthily
As any ear can hear. Come, let's not weep.
If I could shake off but one seven years
From these old arms and legs, by the good gods,
40   I'ld with thee every foot.

CORIOLANUS

Give me thy hand: Come.

Exeunt.

MENENIUS

> That's the best news an ear can hear. Let's not cry now. If my arms and legs were just seven years younger, by the good gods, I'd go with you all the way.

CORIOLANUS

> Give me your hand. Come.

All exit.

ACT 4, SCENE 2

The same. A street near the gate.
Enter the two tribunes, SICINIUS, BRUTUS, *and an Aedile.*

SICINIUS

Bid them all home; he's gone, and we'll no further.
The nobility are vex'd, whom we see have sided
In his behalf.

BRUTUS

               Now we have shown our power,
5   Let us seem humbler after it is done
Than when it was a-doing.

SICINIUS

                     Bid them home:
Say their great enemy is gone, and they
Stand in their ancient strength.

BRUTUS

10   Dismiss them home.

                         Exit Aedile.

Here comes his mother.

Enter VOLUMNIA, VIRGILLA, *and* MENENIUS.

SICINIUS

Let's not meet her.

BRUTUS

Why?

SICINIUS

They say she's mad.

BRUTUS

15   They have ta'en note of us: keep on your way.

VOLUMNIA

O, ye're well met: the hoarded plague o' the gods
Requite your love!

ACT 4, SCENE 2

The same street, near the gate.
SICINIUS, BRUTUS, *and an Aedile enter.*

SICINIUS

Tell them all to go home. He's gone, and we won't go any further. The nobles who sided with him are angry.

BRUTUS

Now that we've exerted our power, let's at least pretend to be humble, like before.

SICINIUS

Tell them to go home. Explain that their great enemy is gone and that their freedoms have been restored.

BRUTUS

Send them home.

The aedile exits.

Here comes his mother.

VOLUMNIA, VIRGILIA, *and* MENENIUS *enter.*

SICINIUS

Let's not talk to her.

BRUTUS

Why not?

SICINIUS

They say she's crazy.

BRUTUS

They've seen us. Keep walking.

VOLUMNIA

Some coincidence, running into you. May the gods repay you for this with the plague!

MENENIUS
                    Peace, peace; be not so loud.

VOLUMNIA
        If that I could for weeping, you should hear,—
20   Nay, and you shall hear some.
        (to SICINIUS*)* Will you be gone?

VIRGILIA
        (to BRUTUS*)* You shall stay too: I would I had the power
        To say so to my husband.

SICINIUS
        (to VOLUMNIA)   Are you mankind?

VOLUMNIA
25   Ay, fool; is that a shame? Note but this fool.
        Was not a man my father? Hadst thou foxship
        To banish him that struck more blows for Rome
        Than thou hast spoken words?

SICINIUS
                                    O blessed heavens!

VOLUMNIA
30   More noble blows than ever thou wise words;
        And for Rome's good. I'll tell thee what; yet go:
        Nay, but thou shalt stay too: I would my son
        Were in Arabia, and thy tribe before him,
        His good sword in his hand.

SICINIUS
35   What then?

VIRGILIA
                                    What then?
        He'ld make an end of thy posterity.

VOLUMNIA
        Bastards and all.
        Good man, the wounds that he does bear for Rome!

MENENIUS
40   Come, come, peace.

MENENIUS

> Calm down. Don't be so loud.

VOLUMNIA

> If I could cry quietly I would. You should hear me cry—
> no, you will hear me. *(to* SICINIUS*)* Where are you going?

VIRGILIA

> *(to* BRUTUS*)* You stay, too. I wish I had the power to say
> that to my husband.

SICINIUS

> *(to* VOLUMNIA*)* Are you a woman?

VOLUMNIA

> You fool, are you trying to insult me? Listen, fool. Wasn't
> my father a man? Are you so ungrateful that you'd banish
> the man who swung his sword for Rome more times than
> you've even opened your mouth to speak?

SICINIUS

> Oh, blessed heavens!

VOLUMNIA

> He fought nobly for Rome more times than you've
> ever spoken wise words. I'll tell you what: go! No, stay
> actually. I wish my son were in the lawless deserts of
> Arabia, with his sword in hand, and your people stood
> before him.

SICINIUS

> What would happen then?

VIRGILIA

> What would happen? He'd kill you, and your family line
> would end.

VOLUMNIA

> Your bastard children's, too. He's a good man, and he was
> wounded fighting for Rome!

MENENIUS

> Now, now, stay calm.

SICINIUS

> I would he had continued to his country
> As he began, and not unknit himself
> The noble knot he made.

BRUTUS

> > I would he had.

VOLUMNIA

45 > "I would he had"? 'Twas you incensed the rabble:
> Cats, that can judge as fitly of his worth
> As I can of those mysteries which heaven
> Will not have earth to know.

BRUTUS

> (*to* SICINIUS) Pray, let us go.

VOLUMNIA

50 > Now, pray, sir, get you gone:
> You have done a brave deed. Ere you go, hear this:—
> As far as doth the Capitol exceed
> The meanest house in Rome, so far my son—
> This lady's husband here, this, do you see—
55 > Whom you have banish'd, does exceed you all.

BRUTUS

> Well, well, we'll leave you.

SICINIUS

> > Why stay we to be baited
> With one that wants her wits?

VOLUMNIA

> > Take my prayers with you.
> > *Exeunt Tribunes.*

60 > I would the gods had nothing else to do
> But to confirm my curses! Could I meet 'em
> But once a-day, it would unclog my heart
> Of what lies heavy to't.

MENENIUS

> > You have told them home;
65 > And, by my troth, you have cause. You'll sup with me?

SICINIUS

I wish he had continued to honor his country the way he always did, rather than renounce his loyalty.

BRUTUS

I wish he had.

VOLUMNIA

"I wish he had"! It was you who incensed the commoners. Those people are like cats and no more able to judge his character than I am able to know the unknowable mysteries of heaven.

BRUTUS

(*to Sicinius*) Please, let's go.

VOLUMNIA

Yes. Please, sir, do go away now. You've done enough. But before you go, hear this: as much as the capitol building stands taller than the lowest house in Rome, that's how much my son, her husband, the man you banished, exceeds all of you.

BRUTUS

That's enough. We're leaving now.

SICINIUS

Why would we stay to be harassed by someone who is clearly out of her mind?

VOLUMNIA

Take my prayers with you.

The tribunes exit.

I wish the gods had nothing else to do but carry out my curses! If I could just meet with them once a day, it would unclog the heavy weight from my heart.

MENENIUS

You've driven them away, and rightly so, I believe. Will you eat with me?

VOLUMNIA
> Anger's my meat; I sup upon myself,
> And so shall starve with feeding.
> (*to* VIRGILIA) Come, let's go:
> Leave this faint puling and lament as I do,
70 In anger, Juno-like. Come, come, come.

They exit.

MENENIUS
> Fie, fie, fie!

He exits.

VOLUMNIA

I'll eat alone. Anger is my meat, but indulging my anger will also be the death of me. (*to* VIRGILIA) Come, let's go. Do as I do: stop whining and being sad. Despite being angry, let's behave like Juno. Come, come, come.

They exit.

MENENIUS

No, no, no!

He exits.

ACT 4, SCENE 3

A highway between Rome and Antium.
Enter a ROMAN *(Nicanor) and a* VOLSCE *(Adrian), meeting.*

ROMAN

I know you well, sir, and you know me: your name,
I think, is Adrian.

VOLSCE

It is so, sir: truly, I have forgot you.

ROMAN

I am a Roman; and my services are, as you are, against
5   'em: know you me yet?

VOLSCE

Nicanor? no.

ROMAN

The same, sir.

VOLSCE

You had more beard when I last saw you; but your favour
is well approved by your tongue. What's the news in
10   Rome? I have a note from the Volscian state, to find you
out there: you have well saved me a day's journey.

ROMAN

There hath been in Rome strange insurrections; the
people against the senators, patricians, and nobles.

VOLSCE

Hath been! is it ended, then? Our state thinks not so: they
15   are in a most warlike preparation, and hope to come upon
them in the heat of their division.

ROMAN

The main blaze of it is past, but a small thing would
make it flame again: for the nobles receive so to heart the
banishment of that worthy Coriolanus, that they are in a
20   ripe aptness to take all power from the people and to pluck
from them their tribunes for ever. This lies glowing, I can
tell you, and is almost mature for the violent breaking out.

ACT 4, SCENE 3

A highway between Rome and Antium.
A ROMAN *(Nicanor) and a* VOLSCE *(Adrian) enter and meet.*

ROMAN

I know who you are, sir, and you know me. I think your name is Adrian.

VOLSCE

That is my name, sir. I'm sorry, but I've forgotten yours.

ROMAN

I'm a Roman, but like you, I work against the Romans. Do you remember me yet?

VOLSCE

Nicanor? No.

ROMAN

That's it, sir.

VOLSCE

You had a fuller beard the last time I saw you, but your speech gives you away. What's happening in Rome? I have instructions from the Volscian state to look for you there. You've saved me a day's journey.

ROMAN

There's been an unusual uprising in Rome: the people against the senators, and nobles.

VOLSCE

Has been? You mean it's over? Our state doesn't think so. They're preparing to attack and hope to surprise them in the middle of the chaos.

ROMAN

Most of it's over, but one small thing would make it erupt again: if the nobles take the news of Coriolanus's banishment so personally that they themselves decide to take all power from the people and do away with their tribunes forever. This could easily happen, and it would definitely lead to violence.

VOLSCE

Coriolanus banished?

ROMAN

Banished, sir.

VOLSCE

25 You will be welcome with this intelligence, Nicanor.

ROMAN

The day serves well for them now. I have heard it said,
the fittest time to corrupt a man's wife is when she's fallen
out with her husband. Your noble Tullus Aufidius will
appear well in these wars, his great opposer, Coriolanus,
30 being now in no request of his country.

VOLSCE

He cannot choose. I am most fortunate, thus accidentally
to encounter you: you have ended my business, and I will
merrily accompany you home.

ROMAN

I shall, between this and supper, tell you most strange
35 things from Rome; all tending to the good of their
adversaries. Have you an army ready, say you?

VOLSCE

A most royal one; the centurions and their charges,
distinctly billeted, already in the entertainment, and to be
on foot at an hour's warning.

ROMAN

40 I am joyful to hear of their readiness, and am the man,
I think, that shall set them in present action. So, sir,
heartily well met, and most glad of your company.

VOLSCE

You take my part from me, sir; I have the most cause to be
glad of yours.

ROMAN

45 Well, let us go together.

Exeunt.

VOLSCE

Coriolanus has been banished?

ROMAN

Banished, sir.

VOLSCE

You'll be welcome with this news, Nicanor.

ROMAN

Things are looking good for the Volsces now. As they say, the best time to seduce another man's wife is when she's in a fight with her husband. Your noble Tullus Aufidius will do well in this attack, since his main enemy, Coriolanus, is no longer fighting for his own country.

VOLSCE

His victory is inevitable. I'm so glad I ran into you. You've told me what I needed to know, and I'll happily accompany you home.

ROMAN

Between now and dinner, I'll tell you all the strange things that are happening in Rome, all of which is good news to her enemies. You said you had an army ready?

VOLSCE

A most royal army. Each officer commands a hundred men, and they are all accounted for and deployable on an hour's notice.

ROMAN

I'm overjoyed to hear that they're ready. I think my report will be what sends them into battle. So glad we met, sir.

VOLSCE

Me, too, sir. I have even more reason to be glad to have met you.

ROMAN

Well, let's go together.

They exit.

ACT 4, SCENE 4

Antium. Before Aufidius's house.
Enter CORIOLANUS *in mean apparel, disguised and muffled*

CORIOLANUS
A goodly city is this Antium. City,
'Tis I that made thy widows: many an heir
Of these fair edifices 'fore my wars
Have I heard groan and drop: then know me not,
5   Lest that thy wives with spits and boys with stones
In puny battle slay me.

Enter a CITIZEN.

Save you, sir.
CITIZEN
And you.
CORIOLANUS
Direct me, if it be your will,
10   Where great Aufidius lies: is he in Antium?
CITIZEN
He is, and feasts the nobles of the state
At his house this night.
CORIOLANUS
               Which is his house, beseech you?
CITIZEN
This, here before you.
CORIOLANUS
15   Thank you, sir: farewell.
                    Exit CITIZEN.

O world, thy slippery turns! Friends now fast sworn,
Whose double bosoms seem to wear one heart,
Whose house, whose bed, whose meal, and exercise,
Are still together, who twin, as 'twere, in love

ACT 4, SCENE 4

In front of Aufidius's house in Antium.
CORIOLANUS *enters in plain clothes, disguised and speaking softly.*

CORIOLANUS

Antium is a good city. I made its women into widows.
Its sons have died at my hands in battle. May I go
unrecognized, so that the women won't spit at me and the
men won't throw stones.

A CITIZEN *enters.*

May the gods protect you, sir.

CITIZEN

And you.

CORIOLANUS

Could you please tell me where to find the great
Aufidius? Is he in Antium?

CITIZEN

He is. The nobles of the state are having a feast at his
house tonight.

CORIOLANUS

Where is his house, do you mind telling me?

CITIZEN

This one, right here.

CORIOLANUS

Thank you, sir. Farewell.

The CITIZEN *exits.*

The world has many twists and turns! Friends who at this
moment are loyal to each other, who seem to share one
heart, live in the same house, sleep in the same bed, eat
the same food, and work together—who love each other

20   Unseparable, shall within this hour,
      On a dissension of a doit, break out
      To bitterest enmity: so, fellest foes,
      Whose passions and whose plots have broke their sleep,
      To take the one the other, by some chance,
25   Some trick not worth an egg, shall grow dear friends
      And interjoin their issues. So with me:
      My birth-place hate I, and my love's upon
      This enemy town. I'll enter: if he slay me,
      He does fair justice; if he give me way,
30   I'll do his country service.

                                                                Exit.

like inseparable twins—will, within an hour, become bitter enemies because of a minor disagreement. And mortal enemies, who spend sleepless nights furiously plotting to capture each other's keep, will by some random chance become dear friends and join their interests together. This is how it is with me: I hate the place I come from and I love my enemy's town. It would be fair for him to kill me, but if he lets me live, I'll fight for his country.

He exits.

level of characters

ACT 4, SCENE 5

Plebias
Virgilia –
lack strong
voices

The same. A hall in Aufidius's house.
Music plays. Enter a SERVINGMAN.

FIRST SERVINGMAN
Wine, wine, wine! What service is here! I think our
fellows are asleep.

Servants happily getting on with
their lowly jobs — unlike in Rome

He exits.

Enter a second SERVINGMAN.

SECOND SERVINGMAN
Where's Cotus? my master calls for him. Cotus!

Obeying every word

He exits.

Enter CORIOLANUS.

CORIOLANUS — ALONE - ∴ audience a

A goodly house: the feast smells well; but I
5   Appear not like a guest.   *why does he do this?*
dramatic irony

Re-enter the first SERVINGMAN.

FIRST SERVINGMAN   *doesn't recognise*
What would you have, friend? whence are you?   *him*
Here's no place for you: pray, go to the door.

He exits.

CORIOLANUS
I have deserved no better entertainment,
In being Coriolanus.

It wouldn't be differe
why – past
play

Re-enter second SERVINGMAN.

ACT 4, SCENE 5

A hall in Aufidius's house.
Music plays offstage. A SERVANT *enters.*

FIRST SERVANT

Wine, wine, wine! What kind of service is this? I think the other servants are asleep.

He exits.

A SECOND SERVANT *enters.*

SECOND SERVANT

Where's Cotus? My master calls for him. Cotus!

He exits.

CORIOLANUS *enters.*

CORIOLANUS

This is a good house. The feast smells good, but I don't look like a guest.

The FIRST SERVANT *reenters.*

FIRST SERVANT

What are you doing here, friend? Where are you from? This is no place for you. Please leave.

He exits.

CORIOLANUS

I wouldn't be welcomed any better if they knew I were Coriolanus. *why wouldn't he?*

The SECOND SERVANT *reenters.*

SECOND SERVINGMAN

10   Whence are you, sir? Has the porter his eyes in his head;
that he gives entrance to such companions? Pray, get
you out.

CORIOLANUS

Away!

SECOND SERVINGMAN

Away! get you away.

CORIOLANUS

15   Now thou'rt troublesome.

SECOND SERVINGMAN

Are you so brave? I'll have you talked with anon.

Enter a THIRD SERVINGMAN. *The first meets him.*

THIRD SERVINGMAN

What fellow's this?

FIRST SERVINGMAN

A strange one as ever I looked on: I cannot get him out of
20   the house: prithee, call my master to him.

                                        He steps aside.

THIRD SERVINGMAN

What have you to do here, fellow? Pray you, avoid
the house.

CORIOLANUS

Let me but stand; I will not hurt your hearth.

THIRD SERVINGMAN

What are you?

CORIOLANUS

25   A gentleman.

THIRD SERVINGMAN

A marvellous poor one.

CORIOLANUS

True, so I am.

(handwritten annotations: "bothered about intruder", "pleading plea", "?", "why marvellous", "Polite")

SECOND SERVANT

> Where are you from, sir? Is the porter blind to let someone like you in? Please, get out.

CORIOLANUS

> Go away!

SECOND SERVANT

> You go away!

CORIOLANUS

> You're making trouble.

SECOND SERVANT

> Are you really this arrogant? Someone's going to come reprimand you right away.

A THIRD SERVANT enters. The First meets him.

THIRD SERVANT

> Who's this?

FIRST SERVANT

> The strangest man I've ever seen. I can't get him out of the house. Please ask my master to come here.

> > *He exits.*

THIRD SERVANT

> Why are you here, fellow? Please, leave this house.

CORIOLANUS

> Let me stay. I won't cause any harm.

THIRD SERVANT

> Who are you?

CORIOLANUS

> A gentleman.

THIRD SERVANT

> A remarkably poor one.

CORIOLANUS

> That's true. I am poor.

THIRD SERVINGMAN

[polite back.]

Pray you, poor gentleman, take up some other station;
here's no place for you; pray you, avoid: come.

CORIOLANUS

30   Follow your function, go, and batten on cold bits.

[go about your business] *Pushes him away.*

THIRD SERVINGMAN

[refuses]

What, you will not? Prithee, tell my master what a
strange guest he has here.

SECOND SERVINGMAN

And I shall.   **SECOND SERVINGMAN** *exits.*

THIRD SERVINGMAN

Where dwellest thou?   *[trivial — not importe]*

CORIOLANUS   *[short sharp]*

35   Under the canopy.   *[questions and]*

THIRD SERVINGMAN   *[answers]*

Under the canopy?

CORIOLANUS

Ay.

THIRD SERVINGMAN

Where's that?

CORIOLANUS

I' the city of kites and crows.   *[Joking!]*

THIRD SERVINGMAN

40   I' the city of kites and crows! What an ass it is! Then thou
dwellest with daws too?

CORIOLANUS

No, I serve not thy master.

THIRD SERVINGMAN

How, sir? Do you meddle with my master?

CORIOLANUS

Ay; 'tis an honester service than to meddle with thy   *[suggestive double sense]*

45   mistress. Thou pratest, and pratest; serve with thy
trencher, hence!   *[^ commanding language]*

Beats him away. Exit **THIRD SERVINGMAN**.

THIRD SERVANT

Please, poor gentleman, go to some other house. This is not the place for you. Please, get out now.

CORIOLANUS

Be like every other servant: go gorge yourself on cold scraps of food.

He pushes the Third Servant away.

THIRD SERVANT

What won't you do? Please, go tell my master what a strange guest he has here.

SECOND SERVANT

I will.   **SECOND SERVANT** *exits.*

THIRD SERVANT

Where do you live?

CORIOLANUS

Beneath the stars.

THIRD SERVANT

Beneath the stars!

CORIOLANUS

Yes.

THIRD SERVANT

Where's that?

CORIOLANUS

In the city of kites and crows.

THIRD SERVANT

In the city of kites and crows! What a joke this is! Then do you live with the simpletons too?

CORIOLANUS

No, I don't serve your master.

THIRD SERVANT

Oh, sir! Are you trying to mess with my master?

CORIOLANUS

Yes. It's more honest than messing around with your mistress. You babble on and on. Pass the serving platter. Go!

He beats him away. The **THIRD SERVANT** *exits.*

Enter AUFIDIUS *with the* SECOND SERVINGMAN.

AUFIDIUS
Where is this fellow?

SECOND SERVINGMAN
Here, sir: I'ld have beaten him like a dog, but for
disturbing the lords within.

He steps aside.

AUFIDIUS
50 Whence comest thou? what wouldst thou? thy name?
Why speak'st not? speak, man: what's thy name?

CORIOLANUS
If, Tullus, (*removing his muffler*),
Not yet thou knowest me, and, seeing me, dost not
Think me for the man I am, necessity
55 Commands me name myself.

AUFIDIUS
                                        What is thy name?

CORIOLANUS
A name unmusical to the Volscians' ears,
And harsh in sound to thine.

AUFIDIUS
                                    Say, what's thy name?
60 Thou hast a grim appearance, and thy face
Bears a command in't; though thy tackle's torn.
Thou show'st a noble vessel: what's thy name?

CORIOLANUS
Prepare thy brow to frown: know'st thou me yet?

AUFIDIUS
I know thee not: thy name?

CORIOLANUS
65 My name is Caius Martius, who hath done
To thee particularly and to all the Volsces
Great hurt and mischief; thereto witness may
My surname, Coriolanus: the painful service,

distinguished

enraged

AUFIDIUS *enters with the* SECOND SERVANT.

AUFIDIUS

Where is this man?

SECOND SERVANT

Here, sir. I would've beaten him like a dog, but that would've disturbed your guests.

He exits.

AUFIDIUS

Where are you from? What do you want? Your name? Why aren't you speaking? Speak, man. What's your name?

CORIOLANUS

If, Tullus *(unmuffling his voice)*, you don't recognize my voice and you don't recognize me by sight, I must tell you my name.

AUFIDIUS

What is your name?

CORIOLANUS

A name the Volsces don't like to hear, unlike yours.

AUFIDIUS

Tell me, what's your name? Your appearance is harsh and your face looks like a commander's. Even though your clothes are torn, your body looks distinguished. What is your name?

CORIOLANUS

Prepare to frown. Do you know me yet?

AUFIDIUS

I don't know your name. What is it?

CORIOLANUS

My name is Caius Martius. I've done great hurt and mischief to you particularly and to all the Volsces, proof of which is my surname: Coriolanus. I worked very hard,

because he fought

betrayed

The extreme dangers and the drops of blood
70   Shed for my thankless country are requited
      But with that surname; a good memory,   *Given the name*
      And witness of the malice and displeasure
      Which thou shouldst bear me: only that name remains;
      The cruelty and envy of the people,   *turncoats*
75   Permitted by our dastard nobles, who   *Collaborators*
      Have all forsook me, hath devour'd the rest;
      And suffer'd me by the voice of slaves to be
      Whoop'd out of Rome. Now this extremity
      Hath brought me to thy hearth; not out of hope—
80   Mistake me not—to save my life, for if
      I had fear'd death, of all the men i' the world
      I would have 'voided thee, but in mere spite,   *Revenge*
      To be full quit of those my banishers, *evicted*
      Stand I before thee here. Then if thou hast   *against*
85   A heart of wreak in thee, that wilt revenge
      Thine own particular wrongs and stop those maims
      Of shame seen through thy country, speed
      thee straight,
      And make my misery serve thy turn: so use it
90   That my revengeful services may prove   *plagued*
disease As benefits to thee, for I will fight   *corrupt*
  +   Against my canker'd country with the spleen
morals Of all the under fiends. But if so be
      Thou darest not this and that to prove more fortunes
95   Thou'rt tired, then, in a word, I also am
      Longer to live most weary, and present
      My throat to thee and to thy ancient malice;   *Spite*
      Which not to cut would show thee but a fool,
      Since I have ever follow'd thee with hate,
100   Drawn tuns of blood out of thy country's breast,
      And cannot live but to thy shame, unless
      It be to do thee service.

Does he tell the truth

faced extreme dangers, and shed drops of blood for my ungrateful country. My only compensation is that name. It's a reminder and signifier of the hatred you should feel for me. That name is all that is left. With envious cruelty, the Roman people, enabled by the cowardly nobles, have turned on me and taken away all that I had. These slaves have voted me out of Rome. These extreme circumstances are what have brought me to your home. Make no mistake: I have no wish to save my life. If I feared death, I would have avoided you more than any other man in the world. Instead I stand here before you with only my hatred and desire for revenge against my banishers. If you're inclined to seek vengeance of your own and end the shame that's seen throughout your country, see now how you can use my suffering to serve your purpose. Helping me get revenge will be beneficial to you. I'll fight my own cursed country with the fury of all the hell beings. But if you choose not to do this, if you're too tired to take this chance, then since I am also too tired to keep living, I present my throat to you and your longstanding hatred. You'd be a fool not to cut it. I've always pursued you with hatred, I've spilled barrels of your country's blood, so to let me live would only bring you shame unless I can work on your behalf.

AUFIDIUS

              O Martius, Martius!
Each word thou hast spoke hath weeded from my heart

105   A root of ancient envy. If Jupiter
Should from yond cloud speak divine things,
And say 'Tis true, I'd not believe them more
Than thee, all noble Martius. Let me twine
Mine arms about that body, where against

110   My grained ash an hundred times hath broke
And scarr'd the moon with splinters.

They embrace.

                       Here I clip
The anvil of my sword, and do contest
As hotly and as nobly with thy love

115   As ever in ambitious strength I did
Contend against thy valour. Know thou first,
I loved the maid I married; never man
Sigh'd truer breath; but that I see thee here,
Thou noble thing! more dances my rapt heart

120   Than when I first my wedded mistress saw
Bestride my threshold. Why, thou Mars, I tell thee,
We have a power on foot; and I had purpose
Once more to hew thy target from thy brawn,
Or lose mine arm for 't: thou hast beat me out

125   Twelve several times, and I have nightly since
Dreamt of encounters 'twixt thyself and me;
We have been down together in my sleep,
Unbuckling helms, fisting each other's throat,
And waked half dead with nothing. Worthy Martius,

130   Had we no quarrel else to Rome, but that
Thou art thence banish'd, we would muster all
From twelve to seventy, and pouring war
Into the bowels of ungrateful Rome,
Like a bold flood o'er-bear 't. O, come, go in,

135   And take our friendly senators by the hands;
Who now are here, taking their leaves of me,

AUFIDIUS

Oh, Martius, Martius! Each word that you've spoken
has weeded from my heart a root of longstanding hatred.
If from that far cloud Jupiter should speak divine things
and say, "It's true," I would believe him no less than I
believe you, noble Martius. Let me wrap my arms around
this body of yours, which my wooden lance has beaten
and been splintered against a hundred times.

They embrace.

You are the anvil that my sword used to strike, and now
I embrace you. Now I strive to gain your comradeship
with as much ferocity and honor as I used to fight you.
You should know: I loved the woman I married, that's
the truth, but seeing you here, you noble thing, makes
my heart more enraptured than when I first saw my new
bride walk across my threshold. You are the god of war!
I tell you, our army is ready to deploy, and now I have
reason again to force your shield off your strong arm,
or lose my own arm instead. You've defeated me twelve
different times, and every night since I have dreamed of
encounters between us. We'd fight down on the ground,
taking off our helmets, forcing our fists into each other's
throats. Then I wake up, half dead, and it was all a dream.
Worthy Martius, even if we had no reason to attack Rome
other than the fact that you've been banished, we would
assemble every man from ages twelve to seventy and
flood ungrateful Rome with our fury. Come inside now
and shake hands with our senators. They are just now
saying goodbye to me, as I was about to attack Roman
territories, though not Rome itself.

Who am prepared against your territories,
Though not for Rome itself.

CORIOLANUS

                        You bless me, gods!

AUFIDIUS

140   Therefore, most absolute sir, if thou wilt have *army*
The leading of thine own revenges, take
The one half of my commission; and set down— *give him to...*
As best thou art experienced, since thou know'st
Thy country's strength and weakness,—thine own ways;
145 Whether to knock against the gates of Rome, } *decision to Coriolan*
Or rudely visit them in parts remote, } *to Coriolan*
To fright them ere destroy. But come in: *sneak in*
Let me commend thee first to those that shall
Say yea to thy desires. A thousand welcomes!
150 And more a friend than e'er an enemy;
Yet, Martius, that was much. Your hand: most welcome!

          Exeunt CORIOLANUS *and* AUFIDIUS.
          The two Servingmen come forward.

FIRST SERVINGMAN

Here's a strange alteration!) *things have changed*

SECOND SERVINGMAN

By my hand, I had thought to have strucken him with a
cudgel; and yet my mind gave me his clothes made a false
155 report of him.

FIRST SERVINGMAN

What an arm he has! he turned me about with his finger
and his thumb, as one would set up a top.

SECOND SERVINGMAN

Nay, I knew by his face that there was something in him:
he had, sir, a kind of face, methought,—I cannot tell how
160 to term it.

FIRST SERVINGMAN

He had so; looking as it were—would I were hanged, but
I thought there was more in him than I could think.

Servants discuss their change of view

CORIOLANUS

You bless me, gods!

AUFIDIUS

Incomparable sir, if you'd like to take the lead with your own revenge, take over half of my command. Because you have the most experience and you know Rome's strengths and weaknesses, decide for yourself whether to attack the city directly at the gates or to sneak up on them in the faraway territories and frighten them before destroying them. Either way, come in. Let me introduce you to those who will approve of your desires. A thousand welcomes! You're more of a friend now than you were ever an enemy—and you were a great enemy. Give me your hand—you are most welcome!

CORIOLANUS and AUFIDIUS exit.
The two Servants come forward.

FIRST SERVANT

That was an unexpected turn of events!

SECOND SERVANT

I swear, I had thought about striking him with a club, but I knew his clothes were a disguise.

FIRST SERVANT

What an arm he has! He turned me around with just his finger and his thumb, the way you'd spin a top.

SECOND SERVANT

No, I knew by his face that there was something about him. He had, sir, a kind of face, I thought—I don't know how to describe it.

FIRST SERVANT

He had a kind of face that looked like it was—I can't find the words for the life of me, but I knew there was more to him than I could see.

SECOND SERVINGMAN

So did I, I'll be sworn: he is simply the rarest man i'
the world.

FIRST SERVINGMAN

165   I think he is: but a greater soldier than he you wot one.

SECOND SERVINGMAN

Who, my master?

FIRST SERVINGMAN

Nay, it's no matter for that.

SECOND SERVINGMAN

Worth six on him.

FIRST SERVINGMAN

Nay, not so neither: but I take him to be the
170   greater soldier.

SECOND SERVINGMAN

Faith, look you, one cannot tell how to say that: for the
defence of a town, our general is excellent.

FIRST SERVINGMAN

Ay, and for an assault too.

Re-enter the third Servingman.

THIRD SERVINGMAN

O slaves, I can tell you news—news, you rascals!

FIRST SERVINGMAN AND SECOND SERVINGMAN

175   What, what, what? let's partake!

THIRD SERVINGMAN

I would not be a Roman, of all nations; I had as lieve be a
condemned man.

FIRST SERVINGMAN AND SECOND SERVINGMAN

Wherefore? wherefore?

THIRD SERVINGMAN

Why, here's he that was wont to thwack our general,
180   Caius Martius.

FIRST SERVINGMAN

Why do you say "thwack our general"?

Short sentence
NOT
in-depth
understa—

SECOND SERVANT

So did I. I swear, he is simply the most unique man in the world.

FIRST SERVANT

I agree, but you already know a better soldier.

SECOND SERVANT

Who, my master?

FIRST SERVANT

It's no contest.

SECOND SERVANT

He's worth six of him.

FIRST SERVANT

That's not true. I think he's the better soldier.

SECOND SERVANT

How could anyone ever say who's actually better? For defending towns, our general is excellent.

FIRST SERVANT

Yes, and for attacking them, too.

The Third Servant reenters.

THIRD SERVANT

Oh, slaves, I have news for you—news, you rascals!

FIRST SERVANTAND SECOND SERVANT

What, what, what? Tell us.

THIRD SERVANT

I'd rather be from anywhere than Rome. I'd gladly prefer to be condemned to die.

FIRST SERVANTAND SECOND SERVANT

Why? Why?

THIRD SERVANT

Because Caius Martius, the man who was inclined to thwack our general, is here.

FIRST SERVANT

What do you mean, "thwack our general"?

THIRD SERVINGMAN

I do not say "thwack our general"; but he was always
good enough for him.

SECOND SERVINGMAN

Come, we are fellows and friends: he was ever too hard
185   for him; I have heard him say so himself.

FIRST SERVINGMAN

He was too hard for him directly, to say the truth on't:
before Corioles he scotched him and notched him like a
carbon ado.

SECOND SERVINGMAN

An he had been cannibally given, he might have broiled
190   and eaten him too.

FIRST SERVINGMAN

But, more of thy news.

THIRD SERVINGMAN

Why, he is so made on here within, as if he were son and
heir to Mars; set at upper end o' the table; no question
asked him by any of the senators, but they stand bald
195   before him: our general himself makes a mistress of him:
sanctifies himself with's hand and turns up the white
o' the eye to his discourse. But the bottom of the news
is that our general is cut i' the middle and but one half
of what he was yesterday; for the other has half, by the
200   entreaty and grant of the whole table. He'll go, he says,
and sowl the porter of Rome gates by the ears: he will
mow all down before him, and leave his passage polled.

SECOND SERVINGMAN

And he's as like to do' t as any man I can imagine.

THIRD SERVINGMAN

Do' t! he will do' t; for, look you, sir, he has as many
205   friends as enemies; which friends, sir, as it were, durst
not, look you, sir, show themselves, as we term it, his
friends whilst he's in directitude.

FIRST SERVINGMAN

Directitude! what's that?

THIRD SERVANT

I don't mean "thwack our general," but he could have.

SECOND SERVANT

Come, we're fellows and friends. Caius Martius was always too much for him—I've heard him say so himself.

FIRST SERVANT

He was too much for him directly, to tell the truth. At Corioles he carved him up like a piece of meat.

SECOND SERVANT

If he'd been a cannibal, he might have broiled and eaten him, too.

FIRST SERVANT

But what other news do you have?

THIRD SERVANT

The guests here can't stop talking about him. It's as if he were the son and heir to Mars. He's sitting at the head of the table and none of the senators are asking him any questions—they've all taken their hats off to him. Our general himself treats him like a mistress, touching his hand like a sacred relic, listening with wide-eyed wonder to his every word. But the bottom line is that our general is now half the man he was yesterday. He's given half his power away to Caius Martius and the whole table supports him. He says that he'll go and catch the keeper of Rome's gates by the ears, that he'll mow down whoever stands in his way, leaving a trail behind him.

SECOND SERVANT

And he's as likely to do it as any man I can imagine.

THIRD SERVANT

Do it! He'll do it. Look, sir, he has as many friends as enemies—and his friends can't actually be friends to him while he's in dejectitude.

FIRST SERVANT

Dejectitude! What's that?

THIRD SERVINGMAN

But when they shall see, sir, his crest up again, and the
210   man in blood, they will out of their burrows, like coney
        after rain, and revel all with him.   *Simile*   rabbit

FIRST SERVINGMAN

But when goes this forward?

THIRD SERVINGMAN

To-morrow, to-day, presently; you shall have the drum
struck up this afternoon: 'tis, as it were, a parcel of their
215   feast, and to be executed ere they wipe their lips.

SECOND SERVINGMAN

Why, then we shall have a stirring world again. This
peace is nothing, but to rust iron, increase tailors, and
breed ballad-makers.

FIRST SERVINGMAN

Let me have war, say I; it exceeds peace as far as day
220   does night; it's spritely, waking, audible, and full of vent.
        Peace is a very apoplexy, lethargy; mulled, deaf, sleepy,
        insensible; a getter of more bastard children than war's a
        destroyer of men.

SECOND SERVINGMAN

'Tis so: and as war, in some sort, may be said to be a
225   ravisher, so it cannot be denied but peace is a great maker
        of cuckolds.

FIRST SERVINGMAN

Ay, and it makes men hate one another.   *Rivalry distrust*

THIRD SERVINGMAN

Reason; because they then less need one another. The
wars for my money. I hope to see Romans as cheap as
230   Volscians. They are rising, they are rising.

FIRST AND SECOND SERVINGMAN

In, in, in, in!   *Exeunt.*

Vote for war

THIRD SERVANT

But when they see that his spirits have lifted and that he's
a man in full vitality again, they'll come out of hiding,
like rabbits after a rain, and celebrate with him.

FIRST SERVANT

When will this happen?

THIRD SERVANT

Tomorrow, today, soon. You'll hear the battle drum by
this afternoon. It's like part of their feast and will be
underway before they've wiped their lips.

SECOND SERVANT

Then things will come back to life again here. This peace
does nothing but rust iron and make people become
tailors and singers.

FIRST SERVANT

I say: give me war. It's better than peace the way night is
better than day. It's spritely, waking, loud, and spirited.
Peace is the definition of stagnation, of lethargy. It's
dull, deaf, sleepy, and unfeeling. It creates more bastard
children than wars destroy men.

SECOND SERVANT

It's true. And while war can be said to be seductive in a
sense, it cannot be denied that in times of peace, wives
cheat on their husbands.

FIRST SERVANT

Yes, and it makes men hate one another.

THIRD SERVANT

Because they need one another less. I'd give my money to
have war! I hope the Romans are as cheap as the Volsces. *(A
noise comes from offstage)* They're getting up from the table.

FIRST AND SECOND SERVANTS

In, in, in, in!

All exit.

ACT 4, SCENE 6

Rome. A public place.
Enter SICINIUS *and* BRUTUS.

SICINIUS
We hear not of him, neither need we fear him;
His remedies are tame—the present peace
And quietness of the people, which before
Were in wild hurry. Here do we make his friends
5   Blush that the world goes well, who rather had,
Though they themselves did suffer by't, behold
Dissentious numbers pestering streets than see
Our tradesmen singing in their shops and going
About their functions friendly.

BRUTUS
10   We stood to 't in good time.

Enter MENENIUS.

                       Is this Menenius?

SICINIUS
'Tis he, 'tis he: O, he is grown most kind of late.

BOTH TRIBUNES
Hail sir!

MENENIUS
            Hail to you both!

SICINIUS
15   Your Coriolanus is not much miss'd, but with his friends:
The commonwealth doth stand, and so would do,
Were he more angry at it.

MENENIUS
All's well; and might have been much better, if
He could have temporized.

SICINIUS
20   Where is he, hear you?

ACT 4, SCENE 6

A Public Place in Rome
The tribunes SICINIUS *and* BRUTUS *enter.*

SICINIUS

We haven't heard about him, so we don't need to fear
him. It would be easy to deal with him now, given the
peace and quietness of the people, who were in such chaos
before. Now we're making his friends blush because
things are going so smoothly. His friends are the ones who
would've chosen—to their own detriment—to see people
arguing in the streets rather than have our tradesmen
back in their shops and happily doing their jobs.

BRUTUS

We turned things around quickly.

MENENIUS *enters.*

Is this Menenius?

SICINIUS

It's him, it's him. He has become very kind lately.

BOTH TRIBUNES

Greetings, sir!

MENENIUS

Greetings to you both!

SICINIUS

Coriolanus is not missed much by anyone but his friends
now. The people would rise up against him if he were still
angry at them.

MENENIUS

That's good. But things would have gone much better if
he could have compromised.

SICINIUS

Where is he? Have you heard?

MENENIUS

Nay, I hear nothing: his mother and his wife
Hear nothing from him.

Enter three or four CITIZENS.

CITIZENS

The gods preserve you both!

SICINIUS

Good e'en, our neighbours.

BRUTUS

25   Good e'en to you all, good e'en to you all.

FIRST CITIZEN

Ourselves, our wives, and children, on our knees,
Are bound to pray for you both.

SICINIUS

Live, and thrive!

BRUTUS

Farewell, kind neighbours: we wish'd Coriolanus
30   Had loved you as we did.

CITIZENS

Now the gods keep you!

BOTH TRIBUNES

Farewell, farewell.

Exeunt CITIZENS.

SICINIUS

This is a happier and more comely time
Than when these fellows ran about the streets,
35   Crying confusion.

BRUTUS

Caius Martius was
A worthy officer i' the war; but insolent,
O'ercome with pride, ambitious past all thinking,
Self-loving—

MENENIUS

No, I hear nothing. His mother and his wife hear nothing from him.

Three or four CITIZENS *enter.*

CITIZENS

The gods preserve you both!

SICINIUS

Good evening, neighbors.

BRUTUS

Good evening to you all, good evening to you all.

FIRST CITIZEN

Ourselves, our wives, and children, on our knees, keep you both in our prayers.

SICINIUS

Live and thrive!

BRUTUS

Farewell, kind neighbors. We wished Coriolanus had cared for you as much as we do.

CITIZENS

Now the gods keep you!

BOTH TRIBUNES

Farewell, farewell.

The CITIZENS *exit.*

SICINIUS

This is a happier and more pleasant time than when the people ran in the streets, shouting their wild demands.

BRUTUS

Caius Martius was a brave officer in the war, but he was stubborn, overcome with pride, unreasonably ambitious, narcissistic . . .

SICINIUS

40   And affecting one sole throne,
          Without assistance.

MENENIUS

          I think not so.

SICINIUS

          We should by this, to all our lamentation,
          If he had gone forth consul, found it so.

BRUTUS

45   The gods have well prevented it, and Rome
          Sits safe and still without him.

          Enter an Aedile.

AEDILE

                              Worthy tribunes,
          There is a slave, whom we have put in prison,
          Reports, the Volsces with two several powers
50   Are enter'd in the Roman territories,
          And with the deepest malice of the war
          Destroy what lies before 'em.

MENENIUS

                              'Tis Aufidius,
          Who, hearing of our Martius's banishment,
55   Thrusts forth his horns again into the world;
          Which were inshell'd when Martius stood for Rome,
          And durst not once peep out.

SICINIUS

          Come, what talk you of Martius?

BRUTUS

          Go see this rumourer whipp'd. It cannot be
60   The Volsces dare break with us.

MENENIUS

                              Cannot be?
          We have record that very well it can,
          And three examples of the like have been

SICINIUS

> And he thought there should be only one governing body without any counterbalancing powers.

MENENIUS

> I don't think that's so.

SICINIUS

> If despite our protests he had become consul, we would know this to be true by now.

BRUTUS

> The gods have skillfully prevented it, and Rome sits safe and sound without him.

An Aedile enters.

AEDILE

> Worthy tribunes, we've just put a slave in prison who says that the Volsces, in two separate armies, have entered Roman territories and are furiously destroying everything in sight.

MENENIUS

> It's Aufidius. Hearing of Martius's banishment, he's thrusting his horns into the world again. When Martius defended Rome, Aufidius was contained and didn't once dare to strike out.

SICINIUS

> Why are you talking about Martius now?

BRUTUS

> Go stop this rumor. The Volsces can't have dared to break our peace treaty.

MENENIUS

> They can't? We've seen many times that they very well can, three times within my own lifetime in fact. Talk

Within my age. But reason with the fellow,
65   Before you punish him, where he heard this,
Lest you shall chance to whip your information
And beat the messenger who bids beware
Of what is to be dreaded.

SICINIUS

                                    Tell not me:
70   I know this cannot be.

BRUTUS

                              Not possible.

Enter a MESSENGER.

MESSENGER

The nobles in great earnestness are going
All to the senate house: some news is come
That turns their countenances.

SICINIUS

75   'Tis this slave—
Go whip him, 'fore the people's eyes:—his raising;
Nothing but his report.

MESSENGER

                              Yes, worthy sir,
The slave's report is seconded; and more,
80   More fearful, is deliver'd.

SICINIUS

                                    What more fearful?

MESSENGER

It is spoke freely out of many mouths—
How probable I do not know—that Martius,
Join'd with Aufidius, leads a power 'gainst Rome,
85   And vows revenge as spacious as between
The young'st and oldest thing.

SICINIUS

                                    This is most likely!

with the prisoner before you beat him. Find out where he heard this. Don't run the risk of punishing the informant who warns you of dreaded news.

SICINIUS

Don't tell me what to do. I know this can't be true.

BRUTUS

It's not possible.

A MESSENGER *enters.*

MESSENGER

The nobles are all hurrying to the Senate house. Some news has come that's making them scowl.

SICINIUS

It's this slave. Go whip him in public view. He's incited everyone with his report.

MESSENGER

Worthy sir, the slave's report has been confirmed, and the news is worse than we feared.

SICINIUS

What could be worse?

MESSENGER

Many people, though I don't know how much they actually know, are openly declaring that Martius has joined with Aufidius and is leading an army against Rome and that he vows revenge on everyone alive.

SICINIUS

This is highly likely!

BRUTUS
>Raised only, that the weaker sort may wish
>Good Martius home again.

SICINIUS
90   The very trick on't.

MENENIUS
>This is unlikely:
>He and Aufidius can no more atone
>Than violentest contrariety.

>*Enter a* SECOND MESSENGER.

SECOND MESSENGER
>You are sent for to the senate:
95   A fearful army, led by Caius Martius
>Associated with Aufidius, rages
>Upon our territories; and have already
>O'erborne their way, consumed with fire, and took
>What lay before them.

>*Enter* COMINIUS.

COMINIUS
100   (*to the tribunes*) O, you have made good work!

MENENIUS
>What news? what news?

COMINIUS
>(*to the tribunes*) You have holp to ravish your own
>   daughters and
>To melt the city leads upon your pates,
>To see your wives dishonour'd to your noses,—

MENENIUS
105   What's the news? what's the news?

COMINIUS
>Your temples burned in their cement, and
>Your franchises, whereon you stood, confined
>Into an auger's bore.

BRUTUS

> The weak common people have only been incited in order to welcome Martius home again.

SICINIUS

> It's a trick.

MENENIUS

> That's unlikely. He and Aufidius can't agree on anything other than to fight each other.

A SECOND MESSENGER enters.

SECOND MESSENGER

> You've been called to the Senate. A frightening army, led by Caius Martius together with Aufidius, rages in our territories. They've already overcome everything in their way, burned it, and took whatever was left.

COMINIUS enters.

COMINIUS

> *(to the tribunes)* Oh, this is all your fault!

MENENIUS

> What news do you have? What news?

COMINIUS

> *(to the tribunes)* You've helped to rape your own daughters and melt the city's lead roofs on your own heads, to see your wives dishonored before your own eyes—

MENENIUS

> What's the news? What's the news?

COMINIUS

> Your temples have been burned down to their foundations, and your political power reduced to the size of a pinhole.

MENENIUS

                    Pray now, your news?
You have made fair work, I fear me.—Pray, your news?—
If Martius should be join'd with Volscians,—

COMINIUS

                                                    If?
He is their god: he leads them like a thing
Made by some other deity than nature,
That shapes man better; and they follow him,
Against us brats, with no less confidence
Than boys pursuing summer butterflies,
Or butchers killing flies.

MENENIUS

(*to the* TRIBUNES) You have made good work,
You and your apron-men; you that stood so much
on the voice of occupation and
The breath of garlic eaters!

COMINIUS

He will shake your Rome about your ears.

MENENIUS

As Hercules did shake down mellow fruit.
You have made fair work!

BRUTUS

But is this true, sir?

COMINIUS

Ay; and you'll look pale
Before you find it other. All the regions
Do smilingly revolt; and who resist
Are mock'd for valiant ignorance,
And perish constant fools. Who is 't can blame him?
Your enemies and his find something in him.

MENENIUS

We are all undone, unless
The noble man have mercy.

MENENIUS

Please, give us your news now. You've made your point,
What's your news? If Martius has joined with Volsces—

COMINIUS

If? Then he is their god. He leads them as if he were a
thing made by some other deity than nature, one that
makes stronger men. And they follow him, against us
children, with the confidence of boys pursuing summer
butterflies or butchers killing flies.

MENENIUS

(to the TRIBUNES) This is all your doing, you and the
tradesmen you represent. You who built your power on
the workmen's votes and the wishes of the lower class!

COMINIUS

He'll bring Rome to its knees.

MENENIUS

The city is ready to fall like the ripe fruits Hercules had
to shake down from the trees. You are responsible for all
of this!

BRUTUS

But is this true, sir?

COMINIUS

Yes, and you'll be dead before it's otherwise. All the
regions are revolting. Whoever resists is mocked for their
ignorant courage and then killed as a loyal fool. Who can
blame Martius? Your enemies and his find something
in him.

MENENIUS

We're all doomed unless he has mercy on us.

COMINIUS
                                    Who shall ask it?
                The tribunes cannot do't for shame; the people
                Deserve such pity of him as the wolf
                Does of the shepherds: for his best friends, if they
140   Should say "Be good to Rome," they charged him even
                As those should do that had deserved his hate,
                And therein show'd like enemies.

MENENIUS
                                                'Tis true:
                If he were putting to my house the brand
145   That should consume it, I have not the face
                To say "Beseech you, cease." You have made fair hands,
                You and your crafts! you have crafted fair!

COMINIUS
                                                You have brought
                A trembling upon Rome, such as was never
150   So incapable of help.

BOTH TRIBUNES
                                    Say not we brought it.

MENENIUS
                How? Was it we? We loved him but, like beasts
                And cowardly nobles, gave way unto your clusters,
                Who did hoot him out o' the city.

COMINIUS
155   But I fear
                They'll roar him in again. Tullus Aufidius,
                The second name of men, obeys his points
                As if he were his officer: desperation
                Is all the policy, strength and defence,
                That Rome can make against them.

                Enter a troop of CITIZENS.

COMINIUS

> Who will ask him for mercy? The tribunes are too
> ashamed, the people deserve his pity like the wolf
> deserves the shepherds', and as for his best friends, if
> they were to ask him to "be good to Rome," they would
> be asking of him what his enemies ought to ask, and that
> would make them appear to be his enemies.

MENENIUS

> It's true. If he were about to burn my house, I wouldn't
> be bold enough to say, "I beg you, stop." You and your
> crafty ways! You've crafted a real mess here!

COMINIUS

> You've brought to Rome a panic without remedy like
> never before.

BOTH TRIBUNES

> We didn't bring it.

MENENIUS

> What? How is it our fault? We supported him but, like
> beasts and cowardly nobles, we ceded power to your
> crowds of people who drove him out of the city.

COMINIUS

> But I fear the crowds will incite him again. Tullus
> Aufidius, the second most famous warrior, obeys
> Martius's orders as if he were his officer. Desperation is
> the only defense that Rome can make against them.

A troop of CITIZENS *enter.*

MENENIUS

160   Here come the clusters.
And is Aufidius with him? You are they
That made the air unwholesome, when you cast
Your stinking greasy caps in hooting at
Coriolanus's exile. Now he's coming;
165   And not a hair upon a soldier's head
Which will not prove a whip: as many coxcombs
As you threw caps up will he tumble down,
And pay you for your voices. 'Tis no matter;
If he could burn us all into one coal,
170   We have deserved it.

CITIZENS

Faith, we hear fearful news.

FIRST CITIZEN

For mine own part,
When I said, banish him, I said 'twas pity.

SECOND CITIZEN

And so did I.

THIRD CITIZEN

175   And so did I; and, to say the truth, so did very
many of us: that we did, we did for the best; and
though we willingly consented to his banishment, yet
it was against our will.

COMINIUS

Ye are goodly things, you voices!

MENENIUS

180   You have made good work, you and your cry!
Shall's to the Capitol?

COMINIUS

O, ay, what else?
                                    Exeunt COMINIUS *and* MENENIUS.

SICINIUS

Go, masters, get you home; be not dismay'd:
These are a side that would be glad to have

MENENIUS

Here come the crowds. Is Aufidius with him? You're the ones that made the air unwholesome when you tossed up your stinking greasy caps, hooting at Coriolanus's exile. Now he's coming, and there's not a hair on a soldier's head that won't become a whip. He'll cut off every fool's head that had tossed up a hat to repay you for your votes. If he could burn us all into one coal, we would deserve it.

CITIZENS

Wait, we hear frightening news.

FIRST CITIZEN

At least for me, when I said banish him, I said it out of pity.

SECOND CITIZEN

And so did I.

THIRD CITIZEN

And so did I. In truth, so did most of us. What we did, we did for the best. And though we agreed to his banishment, it wasn't what we wanted.

COMINIUS

You're making excuses for yourselves!

MENENIUS

You've made a mess, you and your pack! Should we go to the capitol?

COMINIUS

Yes, where else?

COMINIUS *and* MENENIUS *exit.*

SICINIUS

Go, masters, get yourselves home. Don't be dismayed. These people are a faction that would happily have these

185 This true which they so seem to fear. Go home,
     And show no sign of fear.

FIRST CITIZEN
     The gods be good to us! Come, masters, let's home. I ever
     said we were i' the wrong when we banished him.

SECOND CITIZEN
     So did we all. But, come, let's home.

                                        Exeunt CITIZENS.

BRUTUS
190 I do not like this news.

SICINIUS
     Nor I.

BRUTUS
     Let's to the Capitol. Would half my wealth
     Would buy this for a lie!

SICINIUS
         Pray, let us go.

                                        Exeunt.

fears come true. Go home, and show no sign of fear.

FIRST CITIZEN

May the gods be good to us! Come, masters, let's go home. I always said we were wrong to banish him.

SECOND CITIZEN

We all did. But come, let's go home.

The CITIZENS *exit.*

BRUTUS

I don't like this news.

SICINIUS

Nor do I.

BRUTUS

Let's go to the capitol. I'd give half my wealth for this to be a lie!

SICINIUS

Let's go.

All exit.

ACT 4, SCENE 7

A camp, at a small distance from Rome.
Enter AUFIDIUS *and his Lieutenant.*

AUFIDIUS
Do they still fly to the Roman?
LIEUTENANT
I do not know what witchcraft's in him, but
Your soldiers use him as the grace 'fore meat,
Their talk at table, and their thanks at end;
5   And you are darken'd in this action, sir,
Even by your own.
AUFIDIUS
                                    I cannot help it now,
Unless, by using means, I lame the foot
Of our design. He bears himself more proudlier,
10   Even to my person, than I thought he would
When first I did embrace him: yet his nature
In that's no changeling; and I must excuse
What cannot be amended.
LIEUTENANT
                                    Yet I wish, sir,—
15   I mean for your particular,—you had not
Join'd in commission with him; but either
Had borne the action of yourself, or else
To him had left it solely.
AUFIDIUS
I understand thee well; and be thou sure,
20   when he shall come to his account, he knows not
What I can urge against him. Although it seems,
And so he thinks, and is no less apparent
To the vulgar eye, that he bears all things fairly.
And shows good husbandry for the Volscian state,
25   Fights dragon-like, and does achieve as soon
As draw his sword; yet he hath left undone
That which shall break his neck or hazard mine,
Whene'er we come to our account.

ACT 4, SCENE 7

A camp, a short distance from Rome.
AUFIDIUS *and his Lieutenant enter.*

AUFIDIUS

Do they still obey the Roman?

LIEUTENANT

I don't know what spell he has them under, but your soldiers pray to him before eating, talk about him throughout their meal, and thank him at the end. And you are being overlooked, sir, by your own men.

AUFIDIUS

I can't help that now, not without risking our plan. He carries himself more proudly, even in front of me, than I thought he would when I decided to join with him. But that's always been his nature, and I have to excuse what can't be changed.

LIEUTENANT

Yet I wish, sir—I mean for you personally—that you hadn't shared your command with him. I wish either that you had been the commander yourself, or else that you had given him the sole command.

AUFIDIUS

I understand. Rest assured that he must answer for what he's done, and he doesn't know what I can accuse him of. While to the naked eye it seems, and he thinks, that he's behaving fairly and that he's taking good care of the Volscian state by fighting like a dragon and achieving victory as soon as he draws his sword, there's something he has failed to do that will break his neck or risk mine, whenever we come to our reconciliation.

LIEUTENANT

Sir, I beseech you, think you he'll carry Rome?

AUFIDIUS

30 All places yield to him ere he sits down;
And the nobility of Rome are his:
The senators and patricians love him too:
The tribunes are no soldiers; and their people
Will be as rash in the repeal, as hasty
35 To expel him thence. I think he'll be to Rome
As is the osprey to the fish, who takes it
By sovereignty of nature. First he was
A noble servant to them; but he could not
Carry his honours even: whether 'twas pride,
40 Which out of daily fortune ever taints
The happy man; whether defect of judgment,
To fail in the disposing of those chances
Which he was lord of; or whether nature,
Not to be other than one thing, not moving
45 From the casque to the cushion, but commanding peace
Even with the same austerity and garb
As he controll'd the war; but one of these—
As he hath spices of them all, not all,
For I dare so far free him—made him fear'd,
50 So hated, and so banish'd: but he has a merit,
To choke it in the utterance. So our virtues
Lie in the interpretation of the time:
And power, unto itself most commendable,
Hath not a tomb so evident as a chair
55 To extol what it hath done.
One fire drives out one fire; one nail, one nail;
Rights by rights falter, strengths by strengths do fail.
Come, let's away. When, Caius, Rome is thine,
Thou art poor'st of all; then shortly art thou mine.

Exeunt.

LIEUTENANT

> Sir, I beg you, do you think he'll conquer Rome?

AUFIDIUS

> Wherever he goes, they yield to him before he begins
> to attack. The young nobles of Rome, the senators,
> and the patricians all support him. The tribunes aren't
> soldiers, and their people will be as quick to reverse their
> judgment of him as they were to throw him out. I think
> he'll be to Rome like the fish hawk is to the fish: the fish
> will submit by its nature. At first he was a noble servant
> to them, but he couldn't handle the honors bestowed
> upon him. Whether it was pride—winning in battle all
> the time always makes men prideful—or whether it was a
> failure of judgment that he was unable to take advantage
> of the opportunities he had, or whether it was just his
> nature not to evolve from wearing the helmet of a soldier
> to the sitting on the cushion of a senator, to command
> peace in the same austere way that he commanded the
> wars. One of these—he has some of each but none in
> their entirety—caused him to be feared and so despised
> that he was banished. But all his merits should stop
> us from listing his faults. Time will tell whether one is
> judged as virtuous. Powerful men think their power is
> praiseworthy, but nothing destroys power faster than
> publicly proclaiming it. One fire burns out another, one
> nail hammers out another nail, and righteousness and
> strength crumble under their own weight. Come, let's go.
> Caius, when Rome is yours, you will be the poorest of
> them all. And then you'll be mine.

> *All exit.*

ACT FIVE
SCENE 1

Rome. A public place.
Enter MENENIUS, COMINIUS, SICINIUS, BRUTUS, *and others.*

MENENIUS

60 No, I'll not go: you hear what he hath said
 Which was sometime his general; who loved him
 In a most dear particular. He call'd me father:
 But what o' that? Go, you that banish'd him;
 A mile before his tent fall down, and knee
65 The way into his mercy: nay, if he coy'd
 To hear Cominius speak, I'll keep at home.

COMINIUS

 He would not seem to know me.

MENENIUS

         Do you hear?

COMINIUS

 Yet one time he did call me by my name:
70 I urged our old acquaintance, and the drops
 That we have bled together. "Coriolanus"
 He would not answer to: forbade all names;
 He was a kind of nothing, titleless,
 Till he had forged himself a name o' the fire
75 Of burning Rome.

MENENIUS

 (to the Tribunes) Why, so: you have made good work!
 A pair of tribunes that have rack'd Rome,
 To make coals cheap,—a noble memory!

COMINIUS

 I minded him how royal 'twas to pardon
80 When it was less expected: he replied,
 It was a bare petition of a state
 To one whom they had punish'd.

ACT FIVE

SCENE 1

A public place in Rome.

MENENIUS, **COMINIUS**, **SICINIUS**, **BRUTUS**, *and others enter.*

MENENIUS

No, I won't go. You heard what his former general
said, the one who loved him most dearly. He called me
father. But so what? Go, you that banished him, and
fall down on your knees a mile before his tent and crawl
to him, begging for mercy. No, if he refused to listen to
Cominius, I'll stay at home.

COMINIUS

He acted as if he didn't know me.

MENENIUS

Do you hear?

COMINIUS

He called me by my name only once, and I reminded him
of our relationship and the blood we've shed together.
He wouldn't answer to "Coriolanus" or any other name.
He was a kind of nothing, titleless, until he had forged
himself a name out of the fire of burning Rome.

MENENIUS

(*to the Tribunes*) Well now, this is all your doing! A
pair of tribunes that have brought down the price of
coal by letting Rome be burned—what a noble way to
be remembered!

COMINIUS

I reminded him how noble it was to grant pardons
when they are least expected. He replied that it was an
insufficient plea from the state that exiled him.

MENENIUS

                                        Very well:
Could he say less?

COMINIUS

I offer'd to awaken his regard
For's private friends: his answer to me was,
5   He could not stay to pick them in a pile
Of noisome musty chaff: he said 'twas folly,
For one poor grain or two, to leave unburnt,
And still to nose the offence.

MENENIUS

For one poor grain or two!
10   I am one of those; his mother, wife, his child,
And this brave fellow too, we are the grains:
You are the musty chaff; and you are smelt
Above the moon: we must be burnt for you.

SICINIUS

Nay, pray, be patient: if you refuse your aid
15   In this so never-needed help, yet do not
Upbraid's with our distress. But, sure, if you
Would be your country's pleader, your good tongue,
More than the instant army we can make,
Might stop our countryman.

MENENIUS

                                        No, I'll not meddle.
20

SICINIUS

Pray you, go to him.

MENENIUS

What should I do?

BRUTUS

Only make trial what your love can do
For Rome, towards Martius.

MENENIUS

                                        Well, and say that Martius
25   Return me, as Cominius is return'd, unheard;

MENENIUS

That's fair for him to say.

COMINIUS

I tried to make him think of his personal friends. His answer to me was that he couldn't stop to pick them out from a pile of offensive, musty chaff. He said it was foolish to spare one or two poor grains from being burned and still smell the stink.

MENENIUS

For one poor grain or two! I am one of those. His mother, his wife, his child, and this brave fellow, too—we are the grains. You are the musty chaff. Your stink can be smelled above the moon, and we must be burnt for you.

SICINIUS

No, please, be patient. If you refuse to help when it's most needed, don't lecture us while we're in distress. If you'd plead on your country's behalf, surely your good words would do more to stop our countryman than any army we could raise.

MENENIUS

No, I won't get involved.

SICINIUS

Please, go to him.

MENENIUS

What would I do?

BRUTUS

See what your kindness toward Martius can do for Rome.

MENENIUS

All right, but what if Martius sends me back without listening to me, as he did with Cominius? What then?

What then? But as a discontented friend,
Grief-shot with his unkindness? say 't be so?

SICINIUS

Yet your good will
must have that thanks from Rome, after the measure
As you intended well.

MENENIUS

                                        I'll undertake 't:
I think he'll hear me. Yet, to bite his lip
And hum at good Cominius, much unhearts me.
He was not taken well; he had not dined:
The veins unfill'd, our blood is cold, and then
We pout upon the morning, are unapt
To give or to forgive; but when we have stuff'd
These and these conveyances of our blood
With wine and feeding, we have suppler souls
Than in our priest-like fasts: therefore I'll watch him
Till he be dieted to my request,
And then I'll set upon him.

BRUTUS

You know the very road into his kindness,
And cannot lose your way.

MENENIUS

                                        Good faith, I'll prove him,
Speed how it will. I shall ere long have knowledge
Of my success.

                                                    He exits.

COMINIUS

                            He'll never hear him.

SICINIUS

                                                        Not?

COMINIUS

I tell you, he does sit in gold, his eye
Red as 'twould burn Rome; and his injury
The jailer to his pity. I kneel'd before him;

I'll come back simply as a disappointed friend, grief-stricken with his unkindness? What if that happens?

SICINIUS

No, Rome will thank you for your efforts because you have good intentions.

MENENIUS

I'll try. I think he'll listen to me. But it discourages me that he bit his lip and ignored good Cominius. Martius wasn't approached skillfully—he hadn't eaten. When the veins are empty, our blood is cold, and then our outlook on the day is sour. We are unlikely to give or to forgive. But when we have stuffed ourselves with food and wine, we become more flexible than when we're stiff with hunger. So before I ask him, I'll be sure that he has eaten and is therefore likely to grant my request.

BRUTUS

You know exactly how to access his kindness. You can't fail.

MENENIUS

Have faith. Whatever happens, I'll try to convince him. I'll know soon enough whether I have succeeded.

He exits.

COMINIUS

Martius will never listen to him.

SICINIUS

No?

COMINIUS

I tell you, he's sitting on a golden throne, and his eyes are red enough to burn Rome, and his feeling of having been wronged overwhelms his pity. I knelt before him, and he

'Twas very faintly he said "Rise;" dismiss'd me
55   Thus, with his speechless hand: what he would do,
He sent in writing after me; what he would not,
Bound with an oath to yield to his conditions:
So that all hope is vain.
Unless his noble mother, and his wife;
60   Who, as I hear, mean to solicit him
For mercy to his country. Therefore, let's hence,
And with our fair entreaties haste them on.

Exeunt.

very quietly said, "Rise," and without a word, he waved for me to leave. He sent me a letter saying what he will do, and he has sworn not to yield on his conditions. There is no hope unless, as I hear, his noble mother and his wife are able to convince him to have mercy on his country. So let's go then and urge them to hurry.

All exit.

ACT 5, SCENE 2

Entrance of the Volscian camp before Rome.
Two Sentinels on guard.
Enter MENENIUS.

FIRST SENTINEL

Stay: whence are you?

SECOND SENTINEL

Stand, and go back.

MENENIUS

You guard like men; 'tis well: but, by your leave,
I am an officer of state, and come
To speak with Coriolanus.

FIRST SENTINEL

From whence?

MENENIUS

From Rome.

FIRST SENTINEL

You may not pass, you must return: our general
Will no more hear from thence.

SECOND SENTINEL

You'll see your Rome embraced with fire before
You'll speak with Coriolanus.

MENENIUS

Good my friends,
If you have heard your general talk of Rome,
And of his friends there, it is lots to blanks,
My name hath touch'd your ears. It is Menenius.

FIRST SENTINEL

Be it so; go back: the virtue of your name
Is not here passable.

MENENIUS

I tell thee, fellow,
The general is my lover: I have been
The book of his good acts, whence men have read

ACT 5, SCENE 2

An advanced post of the Volscian camp, outside Rome.
Two guards at their station.
MENENIUS *enters.*

FIRST GUARD

Halt! Who are you?

SECOND GUARD

Stop and go back.

MENENIUS

You're good guards, but I assure you that I'm an officer of the state, and I've come to speak with Coriolanus.

FIRST GUARD

Where are you from?

MENENIUS

From Rome.

FIRST GUARD

You may not pass. You must return. Our general won't listen to Romans anymore.

SECOND GUARD

You'll see your Rome consumed with fire before you'll speak with Coriolanus.

MENENIUS

Good men, if you've heard your general talk of Rome and of his friends there, you've undoubtedly heard my name: Menenius.

FIRST GUARD

Even if that's true, go back. You can't get in here by virtue of your name.

MENENIUS

I tell you, fellow, the general is my close friend. I've recorded his brave acts and proclaimed, perhaps exaggeratedly, his greatness as unparalleled. I've always

His name unparallel'd, haply amplified;
For I have ever verified my friends,
Of whom he's chief, with all the size that verity
Would without lapsing suffer: nay, sometimes,
25   Like to a bowl upon a subtle ground,
I have tumbled past the throw; and in his praise
Have almost stamp'd the leasing: therefore, fellow,
I must have leave to pass.

FIRST SENTINEL

Faith, sir, if you had told as many lies in his behalf as
30   you have uttered words in your own, you should not
pass here; no, though it were as virtuous to lie as to live
chastely. Therefore, go back.

MENENIUS

Prithee, fellow, remember my name is Menenius, always
factionary on the party of your general.

SECOND SENTINEL

35   Howsoever you have been his liar, as you say you have, I
am one that, telling true under him, must say, you cannot
pass. Therefore, go back.

MENENIUS

Has he dined, canst thou tell? for I would not speak with
him till after dinner.

FIRST SENTINEL

40   You are a Roman, are you?

MENENIUS

I am, as thy general is.

FIRST SENTINEL

Then you should hate Rome, as he does. Can you, when
you have pushed out your gates the very defender of
them, and, in a violent popular ignorance, given your
45   enemy your shield, think to front his revenges with the
easy groans of old women, the virginal palms of your
daughters, or with the palsied intercession of such a
decayed dotant as you seem to be? Can you think to blow
out the intended fire your city is ready to flame in, with

supported my friends, of whom he's the closest, with the highest possible praise I could give without slipping into lies. Although it's true that sometimes, like bowling on an uneven surface, I've thrown the ball too far and nearly praised him beyond his actual accomplishments. So you see, fellow, you must let me pass.

FIRST GUARD

Sir, if you've told as many lies on his behalf as you've spoken words that benefit yourself, you should not pass here. You act as if it were as virtuous to lie as it is to live honestly. Go back.

MENENIUS

Please, fellow, remember my name is Menenius, and I've always been on your general's side.

SECOND GUARD

Even if you've lied for him, as you say you have, I must follow his orders truthfully and say that you cannot pass. So go back.

MENENIUS

Has he eaten yet, could you tell me? Because I wouldn't want to speak with him until after dinner.

FIRST GUARD

You're a Roman, are you?

MENENIUS

I am, just as your general is.

FIRST GUARD

Then you should hate Rome the way he does. You've banished your greatest hero from your gates and, in a violent popular ignorance, given your best defender to your enemy. So how can you think to counteract his plan for revenge with the meaningless groans of old women, the prayers of your virgin daughters, or the crippled pleas of a decayed, senile old man such as yourself? You think you can blow out the fire that is about to engulf

50   such weak breath as this? No, you are deceived; therefore,
        back to Rome, and prepare for your execution: you are
        condemned, our general has sworn you out of reprieve
        and pardon.

MENENIUS

        Sirrah, if thy captain knew I were here, he would use me
55   with estimation.

SECOND SENTINEL

        Come, my captain knows you not.

MENENIUS

        I mean, thy general.

FIRST SENTINEL

        My general cares not for you. Back, I say, go; lest I let
        forth your half-pint of blood; back,—that's the utmost of
60   your having: back.

MENENIUS

        Nay, but, fellow, fellow—

        Enter CORIOLANUS *and* AUFIDIUS.

CORIOLANUS

        What's the matter?

MENENIUS

        (*to the* FIRST SENTINEL) Now, you companion, I'll say
        an errand for you: You shall know now that I am in
65   estimation; you shall perceive that a Jack guardant cannot
        office me from my son Coriolanus: guess, but by my
        entertainment with him, if thou standest not i' the state of
        hanging, or of some death more long in spectatorship, and
        crueller in suffering; behold now presently, and swoon for
70   what's to come upon thee. (*to* CORIOLANUS) The glorious
        gods sit in hourly synod about thy particular prosperity,
        and love thee no worse than thy old father Menenius
        does! O my son, my son! (*He weeps*) thou art preparing
        fire for us; look thee, here's water to quench it. I was
75   hardly moved to come to thee; but being assured none but

your city in flames with such weak breath as this? If so,
you're mistaken. Go back to Rome and prepare for your
execution. You're condemned, and our general has sworn
to grant you no reprieve or pardon.

MENENIUS

Sirs, if your captain knew that I were here, he would treat
me with respect.

SECOND GUARD

Come, my captain doesn't know you.

MENENIUS

I mean, your general.

FIRST GUARD

My general doesn't care about you. Go back, I say, before
I spill a half pint of your blood. Back, this is as far you
get. Back!

MENENIUS

No, but, fellow, fellow—

CORIOLANUS and AUFIDIUS enter

CORIOLANUS

What's going on?

MENENIUS

(*to the* FIRST SENTINEL) Now, you fellow, I'll give my
version of what just happened here. You'll know now that
I'm well regarded by your general and that a lowly guard
such as yourself can't keep me from Coriolanus, he who is
like a son to me. I wonder if after I talk with him, whether
you'll be hanged or killed more cruelly in some prolonged
and public way. Watch now and worry for what's going
to happen to you. (*to* CORIOLANUS) The glorious gods sit
in hourly discussions about your personal prosperity, and
they love you no less than your old father Menenius does!
Oh, my son, my son! You're preparing fire for us. Look,
here's water to quench it. I was grudgingly persuaded to
come to you, but because they assured me that no one

myself could move thee, I have been blown out of your
gates with sighs; and conjure thee to pardon Rome, and
thy petitionary countrymen. The good gods assuage thy
wrath, and turn the dregs of it upon this varlet here, this,

80   who, like a block, hath denied my access to thee.

CORIOLANUS

Away!

MENENIUS

How! Away?

CORIOLANUS

Wife, mother, child, I know not. My affairs
Are servanted to others: though I owe

85   My revenge properly, my remission lies
In Volscian breasts. That we have been familiar,
Ingrate forgetfulness shall poison, rather
Than pity note how much. Therefore, be gone.
Mine ears against your suits are stronger than

90   Your gates against my force. Yet, for I loved thee,
Take this along; I writ it for thy sake

He gives Menenius a letter.

And would have rent it. Another word, Menenius,
I will not hear thee speak. This man, Aufidius,
Was my beloved in Rome: yet thou behold'st!

AUFIDIUS

95   You keep a constant temper.

Exeunt CORIOLANUS *and* AUFIDIUS.

FIRST SENTINEL

Now, sir, is your name Menenius?

SECOND SENTINEL

'Tis a spell, you see, of much power: you know the way
home again.

FIRST SENTINEL

Do you hear how we are shent for keeping your

100   greatness back?

other than myself could convince you, I've been sent here
from the gates with sighs and beg you to pardon Rome
and your pleading countrymen. May the good gods calm
your anger and turn the remains of it upon this villain
here, who, like a block, has kept me from seeing you.

CORIOLANUS

Away!

MENENIUS

What do you mean, away?

CORIOLANUS

I have neither wife, nor mother, nor child. My personal
life is now eclipsed by other matters. Though I seek my
own revenge, the power to pardon belongs to the Volsces.
We had a friendship, but your ungrateful failure to
defend me has poisoned it. Pity will not remind me of
what great friends we used to be.

So go away. My ears rebuff your pleas with greater force
than your gates will have against my army.

But because I did care for you, take this. I wrote it for
your sake.

He gives Menenius a letter.

And would have sent it. I won't hear you speak another
word, Menenius. This man was my dearest friend in
Rome, Aufidius. But look at him!

AUFIDIUS

You never change.

CORIOLANUS *and* AUFIDIUS *exit.*

FIRST GUARD

Now, sir, is your name Menenius?

SECOND GUARD

You see, it's like a spell with great power. You know the
way home again.

FIRST GUARD

Did you hear how they scolded us for keeping your
greatness back?

SECOND SENTINEL

What cause, do you think, I have to swoon?

MENENIUS

I neither care for the world nor your general: for such
things as you, I can scarce think there's any, ye're so
slight. He that hath a will to die by himself fears it not
105   from another: let your general do his worst. For you, be
that you are, long; and your misery increase with your
age! I say to you, as I was said to, Away!

Exit.

FIRST SENTINEL

A noble fellow, I warrant him.

SECOND SENTINEL

The worthy fellow is our general: he's the rock, the oak
110   not to be wind-shaken.

Exeunt.

SECOND GUARD

Why, do you think, I swoon?

MENENIUS

I don't care about the world or about your general. I
can barely think of things such as yourselves, you're so
insignificant. A suicidal man doesn't fear being killed by
someone else. Let your general do his worst. May you
live long and may your misery increase with age! I say to
you what was said to me: Away!

Exit.

FIRST GUARD

He's a noble fellow, I say.

SECOND GUARD

The worthy fellow is our general. He's like a rock or an
oak that the wind can't shake.

They exit.

ACT 5, SCENE 3

The tent of Coriolanus.
Enter CORIOLANUS, AUFIDIUS, *and others.*

CORIOLANUS
We will before the walls of Rome tomorrow
Set down our host. My partner in this action,
You must report to the Volscian lords, how plainly
I have borne this business.

AUFIDIUS
5   Only their ends
You have respected; stopp'd your ears against
The general suit of Rome; never admitted
A private whisper, no, not with such friends
That thought them sure of you.

CORIOLANUS
10   This last old man,
Whom with a crack'd heart I have sent to Rome,
Loved me above the measure of a father;
Nay, godded me, indeed. Their latest refuge
Was to send him; for whose old love I have,
15   Though I show'd sourly to him, once more offer'd
The first conditions, which they did refuse
And cannot now accept; to grace him only
That thought he could do more, a very little
I have yielded to: fresh embassies and suits,
20   Nor from the state nor private friends, hereafter
Will I lend ear to.

Shout within.
Ha! what shout is this?
Shall I be tempted to infringe my vow
In the same time 'tis made? I will not.

Enter in mourning habits, VIRGILIA, VOLUMNIA, *leading*
young MARTIUS, VALERIA, *and Attendants.*

ACT 5, SCENE 3

Coriolanus's tent.
CORIOLANUS, AUFIDIUS *and others enter.*

CORIOLANUS

Tomorrow we'll lead our army to the walls of Rome. As my partner in this attack, you must report to the Volscian lords on how straightforwardly I've carried this out.

AUFIDIUS

You have respected their aims entirely and blocked your ears against the general plea of Rome. You've never had even a private whisper with your old friends who thought they might persuade you.

CORIOLANUS

This last old man, whom with a broken heart I've sent back to Rome, loved me better than a father. Indeed, he treated me like a god. Their last resort was to send him. Though I turned him away, out of love for him I again offered the same terms they had previously refused and now cannot accept. That is all I have yielded to he who thought that he could do more. I'll no longer listen to any more pleas, made either by the state or by my private friends.

A shout comes from offstage

Ha! What shout is this? Shall I be tempted to break my vow in the same moment that I made it? I will not.

VIRGILIA, VOLUMNIA, *leading young* MARTIUS, VALERIA, *and attendants, enter, in mourning clothes.*

25 My wife comes foremost; then the honour'd mould
Wherein this trunk was framed, and in her hand
The grandchild to her blood. But, out, affection!
All bond and privilege of nature, break!
Let it be virtuous to be obstinate.

VIRGILIA curtsies.

30 What is that curt'sy worth? or those doves' eyes,
Which can make gods forsworn? I melt, and am not
Of stronger earth than others.

VOLUMNIA bows.

My mother bows;
As if Olympus to a molehill should
35 In supplication nod: and my young boy
Hath an aspect of intercession, which
Great nature cries "Deny not." let the Volsces
Plough Rome and harrow Italy: I'll never
Be such a gosling to obey instinct, but stand,
40 As if a man were author of himself
And knew no other kin.

VIRGILIA

My lord and husband!

CORIOLANUS

These eyes are not the same I wore in Rome.

VIRGILIA

The sorrow that delivers us thus changed
45 Makes you think so.

CORIOLANUS

Like a dull actor now,
I have forgot my part, and I am out,
Even to a full disgrace. Best of my flesh,
Forgive my tyranny; but do not say
50 For that "Forgive our Romans."

They kiss.

O, a kiss
Long as my exile, sweet as my revenge!
Now, by the jealous queen of heaven, that kiss

Here comes my wife. Then my mother, the honorable mold from which I was cast. And in her hand, the grandchild of her blood. But affection be gone! And break all natural ties and obligations! Let it be virtuous to be unmovable.

VIRGILLA curtsies.

What is that curtsy worth? Or those doe eyes, which can make the gods break their vows? I melt, and I'm no stronger than anyone else.

VOLUMNIA bows.

For my mother to bow to me is as if Mt. Olympus would plead before a molehill. And my young boy has an imploring look, which by nature I don't want to deny. But let the Volsces destroy Rome and lay siege on Italy—I'll never be so weak as to obey instinct. Instead I will stand firm, as if a man were his own creator and had no family.

VIRGILIA

My lord and husband!

CORIOLANUS

Everything looks different to me since I left Rome.

VIRGILIA

If we look different to you, it's because our suffering has changed us.

CORIOLANUS

Like a bad actor, I have forgotten my lines. To my complete disgrace, I don't know what to say. My dear family, forgive my cruelty but don't ask me to "Forgive our Romans."

VIRGILIA kisses him.

Oh, a kiss as long as my exile, and as sweet as my revenge! By the jealous queen of heaven, I kiss only you, my dear;

I carried from thee, dear; and my true lip
55   Hath virgin'd it e'er since. You gods! I prate,
And the most noble mother of the world
Leave unsaluted: sink, my knee, i' the earth;

He kneels.

Of thy deep duty more impression show
Than that of common sons.

VOLUMNIA

60   O, stand up blest!

He rises.

Whilst, with no softer cushion than the flint,
I kneel before thee; and unproperly
Show duty, as mistaken all this while
Between the child and parent.

She kneels.

CORIOLANUS

65   What is this?
Your knees to me? to your corrected son?
Then let the pebbles on the hungry beach
Fillip the stars; then let the mutinous winds
Strike the proud cedars 'gainst the fiery sun;
70   Murdering impossibility, to make
What cannot be, slight work.

He helps her up.

VOLUMNIA

Thou art my warrior;
I holp to frame thee. Do you know this lady?

CORIOLANUS

The noble sister of Publicola,
75   The moon of Rome, chaste as the icicle
That's curdied by the frost from purest snow
And hangs on Dian's temple: dear Valeria!

VOLUMNIA

(*presenting young Martius*) This is a poor epitome of yours,
Which by the interpretation of full time
80   May show like all yourself.

my lips have always been faithful. You gods! Forgive me
for not saluting the most noble mother of the world.
Sink, my knee, to the earth.

He kneels.

I must demonstrate a more profound sign of my duty
than that of common sons.

VOLUMNIA

Oh, stand up, blessed one!

He rises.

And let me, with no softer cushion than the stone floor,
kneel before you. Though it's inappropriate for me to
pay respect to you—it is the child that should bow to
the parent.

She kneels.

CORIOLANUS

What's this? You're kneeling before me, your chastised
son? Then let the pebbles on the beach rise up the stars
and let the mutinous winds blow the proud cedars into
the fiery sun. Impossible things are now easily possible.

He helps her up.

VOLUMNIA

You're my warrior; I helped make you what you are.
Do you recognize this woman?

CORIOLANUS

The noble sister of the consul Publicola, the moon of
Rome, pure as the icicle that forms from the frost of
purest snow and hangs on Diana's temple: dear Valeria!

VOLUMNIA

(showing young Martius) Here is your miniature replica,
who in time may grow to be exactly like you.

CORIOLANUS
> (*to young Martius*) The god of soldiers,
> With the consent of supreme Jove, inform
> Thy thoughts with nobleness; that thou mayst prove
> To shame unvulnerable, and stick i' the wars
85
> Like a great sea-mark, standing every flaw,
> And saving those that eye thee!

VOLUMNIA
> (*to young Martius*) Your knee, sirrah. *He kneels.*

CORIOLANUS
> That's my brave boy!

VOLUMNIA
> Even he, your wife, this lady, and myself,
90
> Are suitors to you. *Young Martius rises.*

CORIOLANUS
> I beseech you, peace:
> Or, if you'd ask, remember this before:
> The thing I have forsworn to grant may never
> Be held by you denials. Do not bid me
95
> Dismiss my soldiers, or capitulate
> Again with Rome's mechanics: tell me not
> Wherein I seem unnatural: desire not
> To allay my rages and revenges with
> Your colder reasons.

VOLUMNIA
100
> O, no more, no more!
> You have said you will not grant us any thing;
> For we have nothing else to ask, but that
> Which you deny already: yet we will ask;
> That, if you fail in our request, the blame
105
> May hang upon your hardness: therefore hear us.

CORIOLANUS
> Aufidius, and you Volsces, mark; for we'll
> Hear nought from Rome in private.

> *He sits.*

> Your request?

CORIOLANUS

(*to the young Martius*) May the god of soldiers, with the consent of supreme Jove, make your thoughts be noble. And may you be invulnerable to shame, stand firm in the wars like a great beacon for sailors, enduring every sudden blast of wind and helping those that look to you for guidance!

VOLUMNIA

On your knee, sir.

Young Martius kneels.

CORIOLANUS

That's my brave boy!

VOLUMNIA

Even he, your wife, this lady, and myself—plead before you.

Young Martius rises.

CORIOLANUS

Please, stop. Or, if you must ask, remember this first: Don't think that I deny you personally, but I cannot grant your pleas because I have sworn not to. Don't ask me to dismiss my soldiers or to yield to the common people of Rome. Don't tell me the ways in which I seem unnatural. Don't try to mitigate my rage and need for vengeance with your colder reasons.

VOLUMNIA

Oh, no more, no more! You've said you won't grant us anything. We have nothing else to ask other than what you've already refused. But we'll ask that if you fail to grant our request, blame will be laid on your stubbornness. Therefore listen to us.

CORIOLANUS

Aufidius, and you Volsces, come here. We won't listen to anything from Rome in private.

He sits.

What is your request?

VOLUMNIA

Should we be silent and not speak, our raiment
110 And state of bodies would bewray what life
We have led since thy exile. Think with thyself
How more unfortunate than all living women
Are we come hither: since that thy sight,
which should
115 Make our eyes flow with joy, hearts dance
with comforts,
Constrains them weep and shake with fear and sorrow;
Making the mother, wife and child to see
The son, the husband and the father tearing
120 His country's bowels out. And to poor we
Thine enmity's most capital: thou barr'st us
Our prayers to the gods, which is a comfort
That all but we enjoy; for how can we,
Alas, how can we for our country pray.
125 Whereto we are bound, together with thy victory,
Whereto we are bound? alack, or we must lose
The country, our dear nurse, or else thy person,
Our comfort in the country. We must find
An evident calamity, though we had
130 Our wish, which side should win: for either thou
Must, as a foreign recreant, be led
With manacles thorough our streets, or else
triumphantly tread on thy country's ruin,
And bear the palm for having bravely shed
135 Thy wife and children's blood. For myself, son,
I purpose not to wait on fortune till
These wars determine: if I cannot persuade thee
Rather to show a noble grace to both parts
Than seek the end of one, thou shalt no sooner
140 March to assault thy country than to tread—
Trust to' t, thou shalt not—on thy mother's womb,
That brought thee to this world.

VOLUMNIA

Even if we were silent and didn't speak, our clothing and
the condition of our bodies would betray the lives we've
led since your exile. Think how we three are worse off
than all living women, because seeing you—a sight that
should make our eyes flow with tears of joy and our hearts
dance with relief—constrains our eyes from weeping
and shakes our hearts with fear and sorrow to make the
mother, wife, and child see the son, the husband, and
the father tearing his country's bowels out. Your hatred
will kill us poor people. You deny our prayers to the
gods, which is the only comfort we have, and if we can't
pray—and pray for our country—where will we go if
you succeed, where will we go? Alas, either we must
lose the country, our dear mother, or else we must lose
you, our comfort in the country. We will inevitably face
tragedy, but we do have a wish for one side to win. Either
you must, as a traitor, be led with handcuffs thorough
our streets, or else triumphantly march on your ruined
country and wear the medal for having bravely shed your
wife and children's blood. For myself, son, I don't intend
to rely on fortune until these wars end. If I can't persuade
you to reach a noble compromise with both sides rather
than seek total destruction, when you march to assault
your country you'll be treading—and believe me about
this—on your mother's womb, which brought you into
this world.

VIRGILIA

                              Ay, and mine,
            That brought you forth this boy, to keep your name
145   Living to time.

YOUNG MARTIUS

                              He shall not tread on me;
            I'll run away till I am bigger, but then I'll fight.

CORIOLANUS

            Not of a woman's tenderness to be,
            Requires nor child nor woman's face to see.
150   I have sat too long.

                                                  He rises.

VOLUMNIA

                              Nay, go not from us thus.
            If it were so that our request did tend
            To save the Romans, thereby to destroy
            The Volsces whom you serve, you might condemn us,
155   As poisonous of your honour: no; our suit
            Is that you reconcile them: while the Volsces
            May say "This mercy we have show'd"; the Romans,
            "This we received"; and each in either side
            Give the all-hail to thee and cry "Be blest
160   For making up this peace!" Thou know'st, great son,
            The end of war's uncertain, but this certain,
            That, if thou conquer Rome, the benefit
            Which thou shalt thereby reap is such a name,
            Whose repetition will be dogg'd with curses;
165   Whose chronicle thus writ: "The man was noble,
            But with his last attempt he wiped it out;
            Destroy'd his country, and his name remains
            To the ensuing age abhorr'd." Speak to me, son:
            Thou hast affected the fine strains of honour,
170   To imitate the graces of the gods;
            To tear with thunder the wide cheeks o' the air,
            And yet to charge thy sulphur with a bolt
            That should but rive an oak. Why dost not speak?

VIRGILIA

Yes, and mine that gave you this boy, to keep your name alive.

YOUNG MARTIUS

He won't tread on me. I'll run away until I'm bigger, but then I'll fight.

CORIOLANUS

I'll become tender like a woman if I look at your faces. I've sat too long.

He rises.

VOLUMNIA

No, don't leave us now. If our request was to save the Romans and thereby destroy the Volsces, whom you serve, you might condemn us for poisoning your honor. But no, our appeal is for you to reconcile with them so that the Volsces may say, "We have shown mercy," and the Romans may say, "We received mercy," and both sides will salute you and cry, "May you be blessed for making this peace!" You know, great son, that the outcome of war is uncertain. But it's certain that if you conquer Rome, the benefit you'll reap in so doing is a name whose repetition will be plagued with curses. You'll be remembered with these words: "The man was noble, but with his last attack he gave up his nobility, destroyed his country, and his name remains forever hated." Speak to me, son. You've aspired to great honor, to behave like a god, to tear apart the sky with thunder and yet throw your lightning bolt so that it would only split an oak. Why don't you speak?

Think'st thou it honourable for a noble man
175   Still to remember wrongs? Daughter, speak you:
He cares not for your weeping. Speak thou, boy:
Perhaps thy childishness will move him more
Than can our reasons. There's no man in the world
More bound to 's mother; yet here he lets me prate
180   Like one i' the stocks. Thou hast never in thy life
Show'd thy dear mother any courtesy,
When she, poor hen, fond of no second brood,
Has cluck'd thee to the wars and safely home,
Loaden with honour. Say my request's unjust,
185   And spurn me back: but if it be not so,
Thou art not honest; and the gods will plague thee,
That thou restrain'st from me the duty which
To a mother's part belongs.

He turns away.

Down, ladies; let us shame him with our knees.
190   To his surname Coriolanus 'longs more pride
Than pity to our prayers. Down: an end.

They kneel.

This is the last: so we will home to Rome,
And die among our neighbours. Nay, behold 's:
This boy that cannot tell what he would have
195   But kneels and holds up hands for fellowship,
Does reason our petition with more strength
Than thou hast to deny 't. Come, let us go.

They rise.

This fellow had a Volscian to his mother;
His wife is in Corioles and his child
200   Like him by chance. Yet give us our dispatch:
I am hush'd until our city be a-fire,
And then I'll speak a little.

He holds her by the hand, silent.

CORIOLANUS
(*crying*)   O mother, mother!
What have you done? Behold, the heavens do ope,

Do you think it's honorable for a noble man to always
remember how he has been wronged? Daughter, speak—
he doesn't like your weeping. Speak, boy—perhaps your
childishness will move him more than our reasons can.
There's no man in the world more tied to his mother, and
yet here he lets me prattle on like a common criminal.
Never in your life have you done your dear mother any
favors, while she, poor woman, who didn't want to have
another child, has cared for you while you were at war
and safely home, heaped with honors. If you think my
request is unfair, then turn me down. But if it's not, then
you're a liar and the gods will punish you for failing to
give me what you owe me as a son.

He turns away.

Down, ladies. Let's shame him by getting on our knees.
His surname, Coriolanus, has more pride than pity for
our prayers. Down! This is the end.

The women and young Martius kneel.

We'll go home to Rome and die among our neighbors.
Wait, look. This boy, who doesn't know what's going
to happen to him but kneels and holds up his hands for
fellowship, lends more strength to our petition than you
have strength to deny. Come, let's go.

They rise.

This fellow has a Volscian mother, his wife is in Corioles,
and his child looks just like him by chance. Send us away.
I'll be silent until our city is on fire, and then I'll speak a
little.

Coriolanus holds her by the hand, silent.

CORIOLANUS

(*crying*) Oh, mother, mother! What have you done? Look,
the heavens are opening, the gods are looking down

205 The gods look down, and this unnatural scene
They laugh at. O my mother, mother! O!
You have won a happy victory to Rome;
But, for your son—believe it, O, believe it!
Most dangerously you have with him prevail'd,
210 If not most mortal to him. But, let it come.
Aufidius, though I cannot make true wars,
I'll frame convenient peace. Now, good Aufidius,
Were you in my stead, would you have heard
A mother less? or granted less, Aufidius?

AUFIDIUS
215 I was moved withal.

CORIOLANUS
                            I dare be sworn you were:
And, sir, it is no little thing to make
Mine eyes to sweat compassion. But, good sir,
What peace you'll make, advise me: for my part,
220 I'll not to Rome, I'll back with you; and pray you,
Stand to me in this cause. O mother! wife!

                            He speaks with them aside.

AUFIDIUS
(Aside) I am glad thou hast set thy mercy and thy honour
At difference in thee: out of that I'll work
Myself a former fortune.

                    The Ladies make signs to **CORIOLANUS**.

CORIOLANUS
225 (to **VOLUMNIA**, **VIRGILIA**) Ay, by and by;
But we will drink together; and you shall bear
A better witness back than words, which we,
On like conditions, will have counter-seal'd.
Come, enter with us. Ladies, you deserve
230 To have a temple built you: all the swords
In Italy, and her confederate arms,
Could not have made this peace.

                            Exeunt.

and laughing at this unnatural scene. Oh, my mother,
mother! Oh! You have won a happy victory for Rome.
But for your son—believe it, oh, believe it—because you
have convinced him, he's now in mortal danger. But let
it come. Aufidius, though I cannot fight this war for you,
I'll arrange a peaceful settlement, fair to both sides. Now,
good Aufidius, if you were in my place, wouldn't you
have listened to your mother and done as I did, Aufidius?

AUFIDIUS

I was moved by what she said.

CORIOLANUS

I know you were! And, sir, it is no small achievement
to make me cry tears of compassion. But, good sir, tell
me that you'll make peace. For my part, I won't go to
Rome—I'll go back with you. And please, support me in
this effort. Oh, mother! Wife!

He speaks with them aside.

AUFIDIUS

(aside) I'm glad you've distinguished between your mercy
and your honor. I'll be able to rebuild my former fortune
because of that distinction.

The ladies make signs to **CORIOLANUS**.

CORIOLANUS

(to **VOLUMNIA** *and* **VIRGILIA***)* Yes, so it will go. But we'll
drink together, and you'll bring back a signed peace
treaty, not just our word. Come with us. Ladies, you
deserve to have a temple built for you. All the swords of
Italy and her allies couldn't have made this peace.

All exit.

ACT 5, SCENE 4

Rome. A public place.
Enter MENENIUS *and* SICINIUS

MENENIUS

See you yond coign o' the Capitol, yond corner-stone?

SICINIUS

Why, what of that?

MENENIUS

If it be possible for you to displace it with your little
finger, there is some hope the ladies of Rome, especially
5   his mother, may prevail with him. But I say there
is no hope in't: our throats are sentenced and stay
upon execution.

SICINIUS

Is 't possible that so short a time can alter the condition of
a man!

MENENIUS

10   There is differency between a grub and a butterfly;
yet your butterfly was a grub. This Martius is grown
from man to dragon: he has wings; he's more than a
creeping thing.

SICINIUS

He loved his mother dearly.

MENENIUS

15   So did he me: and he no more remembers his mother
now than an eight-year-old horse. The tartness of his
face sours ripe grapes: when he walks, he moves like an
engine, and the ground shrinks before his treading: he is
able to pierce a corslet with his eye; talks like a knell, and
20   his hum is a battery. He sits in his state, as a thing made
for Alexander. What he bids be done is finished with his
bidding. He wants nothing of a god but eternity and a
heaven to throne in.

ACT 5, SCENE 4

A public place in Rome.

MENENIUS *and* SICINIUS *enter.*

MENENIUS

Do you see, beyond the corner of the capitol, beyond the cornerstone?

SICINIUS

What is that?

MENENIUS

If you can block it with your little finger, there is some hope that the ladies of Rome, especially his mother, might prevail with him. But I don't think there is any hope. Our fate is sealed. Our throats wait to be slit.

SICINIUS

Is it possible that a man can change so much in so short a time?

MENENIUS

There's a difference between a caterpillar and a butterfly, but butterflies were once caterpillars. This Martius has grown from man to dragon: he has wings—he's more than a creeping thing.

SICINIUS

He loved his mother dearly.

MENENIUS

He also loved me. He won't remember his mother any more than an eight-year-old horse would. The tartness of his face makes ripe grapes go sour. When he walks, he moves like a war machine, and the ground sinks beneath his feet. He's able to pierce armor with his eye, he talks like a death knell, and his voice itself is an assault. He sits on his throne, looking like a statue of Alexander the Great. His orders are carried out as soon as he gives them. All that he lacks to be a god is immortality and a heaven to rule.

SICINIUS

Yes, mercy, if you report him truly.

MENENIUS

25   I paint him in the character. Mark what mercy his mother
shall bring from him: there is no more mercy in him than
there is milk in a male tiger; that shall our poor city find:
and all this is long of you.

SICINIUS

The gods be good unto us!

MENENIUS

30   No, in such a case the gods will not be good unto us.
When we banished him, we respected not them; and, he
returning to break our necks, they respect not us.

Enter a **MESSENGER**.

MESSENGER

(to **SICINIUS**) Sir, if you'd save your life, fly to your house:
The plebeians have got your fellow-tribune
35   And hale him up and down, all swearing, if
The Roman ladies bring not comfort home,
They'll give him death by inches.

Enter a **SECOND MESSENGER**.

SICINIUS

What's the news?

SECOND MESSENGER

Good news, good news; the ladies have prevail'd,
40   The Volscians are dislodged, and Martius gone:
A merrier day did never yet greet Rome,
No, not the expulsion of the Tarquins.

SICINIUS

Friend,
Art thou certain this is true? is it most certain?

SICINIUS

He lacks the mercy of a god, if you're telling the truth.

MENENIUS

I'm giving a sketch of his character. Let's see how much mercy his mother gets out of him. There's no more mercy in him than there is milk in a male tiger. Our poor city will soon find this out, and it's all because of you.

SICINIUS

May the gods be good to us!

MENENIUS

No, in this case the gods won't be good to us. When we banished him, we dishonored them. And now he's returning to break our necks, which shows that they don't respect us.

A MESSENGER *enters.*

MESSENGER

(*to* SICINIUS) Sir, if you want to save your life, go home immediately. The people have taken custody of your fellow tribune and are hauling him up and down the street, all swearing that if the Roman ladies don't return with a peaceful resolution, they'll torture him to death.

A SECOND MESSENGER *enters.*

SICINIUS

What's the news?

SECOND MESSENGER

Good news, good news! The ladies have prevailed, the Volsces have retreated, and Martius is gone! Rome has never had a happier day. Not even the expulsion of the Tarquins tops this.

SICINIUS

Friend, are you certain this is true? Is it absolutely certain?

SECOND MESSENGER

45   As certain as I know the sun is fire:
       Where have you lurk'd, that you make doubt of it?
       Ne'er through an arch so hurried the blown tide,
       As the recomforted through the gates. Why, hark you!
                Trumpets, hautboys, drums beat, all together.
       The trumpets, sackbuts, psalteries and fifes,
50   Tabours and cymbals and the shouting Romans,
       Make the sun dance. Hark you!
                     A shout within.

MENENIUS

                   This is good news:
       I will go meet the ladies. This Volumnia
       Is worth of consuls, senators, patricians,
55   A city full; of tribunes, such as you,
       A sea and land full. You have pray'd well to-day:
       This morning for ten thousand of your throats
       I'd not have given a doit. Hark, how they joy!
               Music still, with the shouts.

SICINIUS

       (*to* SECOND MESSENGER) First, the gods bless you for your
          tidings; next, accept my thankfulness.

SECOND MESSENGER

60   Sir, we have all great cause to give great thanks.

SICINIUS

       They are near the city?

SECOND MESSENGER

       Almost at point to enter.

SICINIUS

       We will meet them, and help the joy.
                        Exeunt.

SECOND MESSENGER

> As certain as I know the sun is fire. Where have you been that you doubt it? The tide has never blown more quickly through an arch as this reassuring news has blown through the gates. Why, look here!
>
> *Trumpets and pipes sound, drums beat, all together.*
>
> The trumpets, trombones, strings and pipes, drums and cymbals, and the shouting Romans sparkle in the sun. Listen!
>
> *A shout comes from offstage.*

MENENIUS

> This is good news. I'll go meet the ladies. This Volumnia is worth of a city full of consuls, senators, and patricians, and she's worth a sea and land full of tribunes. You have prayed well today. This morning I thought the chance that you'd live was one in ten thousand. Look how happy they are!
>
> *Music still plays, with shouts.*

SICINIUS

> *(to SECOND MESSENGER)* First, may the gods bless you for your good news, and then accept my thanks.

SECOND MESSENGER

> Sir, we have all great cause to give great thanks.

SICINIUS

> Are they near the city?

SECOND MESSENGER

> They're just about to enter.

SICINIUS

> We'll meet them and join the celebration.
>
> *All exit.*

ACT 5, SCENE 5

The same. A street near the gate.
Enter two Senators with VOLUMNIA, VIRGILIA, VALERIA, *&*
their entourage passing over the stage, followed by Patricians
and others.

FIRST SENATOR

Behold our patroness, the life of Rome!
Call all your tribes together, praise the gods,
And make triumphant fires; strew flowers before them:
Unshout the noise that banish'd Martius,
5   Repeal him with the welcome of his mother;
Cry "Welcome, ladies, welcome!"

ALL

Welcome, ladies,
Welcome!

A flourish with drums and trumpets. Exeunt.

ACT 5, SCENE 5

The same street near the gate.
Two Senators enter with VOLUMNIA, VIRGILIA, VALERIA, *and*
their entourage passing over the stage, followed by patricians
and others.

FIRST SENATOR

Behold our savior, the life of Rome! Call all your tribes
together, praise the gods, and make triumphant fires.
Throw flowers before them. Take back the cries that
banished Martius and bring him back by welcoming his
mother. Cry, "Welcome, ladies, welcome!"

ALL

Welcome, ladies, welcome!

Drums and trumpets sound. All exit.

ACT 5, SCENE 6

Antium. A public place.
Enter TULLUS AUFIDIUS, *with Attendants.*

AUFIDIUS

Go tell the lords o' the city I am here:
Deliver them this paper.

> *He gives them a paper.*

Having read it,
Bid them repair to the market-place; where I,
5   Even in theirs and in the commons' ears,
Will vouch the truth of it. Him I accuse
The city ports by this hath enter'd and
Intends to appear before the people, hoping
To purge herself with words: dispatch.

> *Exeunt Attendants.*

Enter three or four Conspirators of AUFIDIUS'S *faction.*

10   Most welcome!

FIRST CONSPIRATOR

How is it with our general?

AUFIDIUS

                        Even so
As with a man by his own alms empoison'd,
And with his charity slain.

SECOND CONSPIRATOR

15   Most noble sir,
If you do hold the same intent wherein
You wish'd us parties, we'll deliver you
Of your great danger.

AUFIDIUS

                    Sir, I cannot tell:
20   We must proceed as we do find the people.

ACT 5, SCENE 6

A public place in Antium.

TULLUS AUFIDIUS *enters, with attendants.*

AUFIDIUS

Go tell the lords of the city that I'm here. Give them
this paper.

He gives them a paper.

Once they've read it, ask them to go to the marketplace.
I'll be there to confirm its truthfulness for them and
for the common people. He whom I accuse has entered
through the city's gates and intends to appear before the
people, hoping to explain himself with words. Hurry.

The attendants exit.

Three or four Conspirators of AUFIDIUS'S *faction enter.*

Most welcome!

FIRST CONSPIRATOR

How are you, general?

AUFIDIUS

Like a man destroyed by his own kindness and killed by
his compassion.

SECOND CONSPIRATOR

Most noble sir, if you still want to work together, we'll rid
you of your great threat.

AUFIDIUS

Sir, I don't know yet. We must see how the people react.

THIRD CONSPIRATOR

The people will remain uncertain whilst
'Twixt you there's difference; but the fall of either
Makes the survivor heir of all.

AUFIDIUS

                                        I know it;
25 And my pretext to strike at him admits
A good construction. I raised him, and I pawn'd
Mine honour for his truth: who being so heighten'd,
He water'd his new plants with dews of flattery,
Seducing so my friends; and, to this end,
30 He bow'd his nature, never known before
But to be rough, unswayable and free.

THIRD CONSPIRATOR

Sir, his stoutness
When he did stand for consul, which he lost
By lack of stooping,—

AUFIDIUS

                              That I would have spoke of:
35 Being banish'd for't, he came unto my hearth;
Presented to my knife his throat: I took him;
Made him joint servant with me; gave him way
In all his own desires; nay, let him choose
40 Out of my files, his projects to accomplish,
My best and freshest men; served his designments
In mine own person; holp to reap the fame
Which he did end all his; and took some pride
To do myself this wrong: till, at the last,
45 I seem'd his follower, not partner, and
He waged me with his countenance, as if
I had been mercenary.

FIRST CONSPIRATOR

                              So he did, my lord:
The army marvell'd at it, and, in the last,
50 When he had carried Rome and that we look'd
For no less spoil than glory—

THIRD CONSPIRATOR

The people won't know how to react if there's no rivalry between you two, but whoever loses leaves the other man with power over everything.

AUFIDIUS

I know, and my reason for attacking him is well founded. I put him in this position of power, and I sacrificed my honor for his loyalty. He became so highly esteemed that he watered his new plants with the dew of flattery. He seduced my friends by changing his nature—he was never known before as anything other than rough, unswayable, and unrestrained.

THIRD CONSPIRATOR

Sir, his stubbornness when he was being considered for consul is why he lost. He wouldn't humble himself.

AUFIDIUS

That's what I was about to say: being banished for his stubbornness, he came to my house and put my knife to his throat. I took him in, made him joint commander of my army, let him do whatever he wanted. I even let him choose men from among my soldiers to carry out his agenda—my best and freshest men. I served his vision myself, helped him do the deeds that he took all the credit for. He wronged me in becoming so prideful. In the end, I looked like his follower, not his partner, and he treated me like I was just a soldier-for-hire.

FIRST CONSPIRATOR

That's what he did, my lord. The army was astonished by it. And finally, when he was able to conquer Rome and we could have had the spoils and glory—

AUFIDIUS

There was it:
For which my sinews shall be stretch'd upon him.
At a few drops of women's rheum, which are
55 As cheap as lies, he sold the blood and labour
Of our great action: therefore shall he die,
And I'll renew me in his fall. But, hark!

Drums and trumpets sound, with great shouts of the People.

FIRST CONSPIRATOR

Your native town you enter'd like a post,
And had no welcomes home: but he returns,
60 Splitting the air with noise.

SECOND CONSPIRATOR

And patient fools,
Whose children he hath slain, their base throats tear
With giving him glory.

THIRD CONSPIRATOR

Therefore, at your vantage,
65 Ere he express himself, or move the people
With what he would say, let him feel your sword,
Which we will second. When he lies along,
After your way his tale pronounced shall bury
His reasons with his body.

AUFIDIUS

70 Say no more.

Enter the Lords of the city.
Here come the lords.

LORDS

You are most welcome home.

AUFIDIUS

I have not deserved it.
But, worthy lords, have you with heed perused
75 What I have written to you?

LORDS

We have.

AUFIDIUS

That's why I'll use all my strength against him. He sold us out, forfeiting the blood and labor of our great plan because of a few drops of women's tears, which are as worthless as lies. Therefore he must die, and I'll reassert my power by taking him down. But look!

Drums and trumpets sound, with great shouts of the people.

FIRST CONSPIRATOR

You returned home like a messenger—you weren't properly welcomed. But he comes back to a loud celebration.

SECOND CONSPIRATOR

And ignorant fools, whose children he has killed, tear their stupid throats as they sing his praises.

THIRD CONSPIRATOR

Seize your opportunity now, before he speaks and convinces the people with whatever he plans to say. Let him feel your sword—we support you. When he lies dead, you can tell the people what he did from your perspective. His version of the story will be buried along with his body.

AUFIDIUS

Say no more.

The Lords of the city enter.

Here come the Lords.

THE LORDS

This celebration welcomes you home.

AUFIDIUS

I don't deserve it. But, worthy lords, have you carefully read the letter I wrote you?

LORDS

We have.

FIRST LORD

And grieve to hear't.
What faults he made before the last, I think
Might have found easy fines: but there to end
Where he was to begin and give away
The benefit of our levies, answering us
With our own charge, making a treaty where
There was a yielding—this admits no excuse.

Enter CORIOLANUS, *marching with drum and colours;*
commoners being with him.

AUFIDIUS

He approaches: you shall hear him.

CORIOLANUS

Hail, lords! I am return'd your soldier,
No more infected with my country's love
Than when I parted hence, but still subsisting
Under your great command. You are to know
That prosperously I have attempted and
With bloody passage led your wars even to
The gates of Rome. Our spoils we have brought home
Do more than counterpoise a full third part
The charges of the action. We have made peace
With no less honour to the Antiates
Than shame to the Romans: and we here deliver,
Subscribed by the consuls and patricians,
Together with the seal o' the senate, what
We have compounded on.

AUFIDIUS

Read it not, noble lords;
But tell the traitor, in the high'st degree
He hath abused your powers.

CORIOLANUS

"Traitor?" How now?

AUFIDIUS

Ay, traitor, Martius!

FIRST LORD

> And we're sad to hear it. Whatever mistakes he made before this last one, I think we could have forgiven with light punishment. But stopping the attack when it was about to begin, squandering the advantage of our army' position, leaving us to pay the cost of raising that army, and making a peace treaty when the enemy was weak and could have been conquered—there's no excuse for this.

> *CORIOLANUS enters, marching with drum and colors; commoners enter with him.*

AUFIDIUS

> Here he comes. You'll hear how he tells it.

CORIOLANUS

> Hail, lords! I have returned as your soldier, no more loyal to my country than when I left here. I remain under your great command. You should know that I have successfully won the bloody battles that brought your army to the gates of Rome. The spoils we've brought home outweigh the bodies of those we killed by more than a third. We've made peace, which brings honor to the people of Antium as much as it shames the people of Rome. And we here present, signed by the Roman consuls and patricians, and with the seal of the Senate, the treaty we've agreed to.

AUFIDIUS

> Don't read it, noble lords. Instead, tell the traitor that he has abused your powers to the highest degree.

CORIOLANUS

> Traitor! How's that?

AUFIDIUS

> Yes, traitor, Martius!

CORIOLANUS
Martius?

AUFIDIUS

105 Ay, Martius, Caius Martius: dost thou think
I'll grace thee with that robbery, thy stol'n name
Coriolanus in Corioles?
You lords and heads o' the state, perfidiously
He has betray'd your business, and given up,
110 For certain drops of salt, your city Rome,
I say "your city," to his wife and mother;
Breaking his oath and resolution like
A twist of rotten silk, never admitting
Counsel o' the war, but at his nurse's tears
115 He whined and roar'd away your victory,
That pages blush'd at him and men of heart
Look'd wondering each at other.

CORIOLANUS

Hear'st thou, Mars?

AUFIDIUS
Name not the god, thou boy of tears!

CORIOLANUS

120 Ha?

AUFIDIUS
No more.

CORIOLANUS
Measureless liar, thou hast made my heart
Too great for what contains it. "Boy"? O slave!
Pardon me, lords, 'tis the first time that ever
125 I was forced to scold. Your judgments, my grave lords,
Must give this cur the lie: and his own notion—
Who wears my stripes impress'd upon him; that
Must bear my beating to his grave—shall join
To thrust the lie unto him.

FIRST LORD

130 Peace, both, and hear me speak.

CORIOLANUS

"Martius"!

AUFIDIUS

Yes, "Martius." Caius Martius. Do you think I'll honor you with that stolen name, Coriolanus, that you took in Corioles? You lords and heads of state, he has treacherously betrayed your mission and given up your city of Rome—and I mean "your city"—because of a few tears from his wife and mother. He has broken his sworn oath like a rotten braid of silk, never following the advice of his fellow officers, but at his mother's tears he cried and gave away your victory. The young attendants blushed and the courageous men looked at each other and wondered what to think.

CORIOLANUS

Do you hear this, Mars?

AUFIDIUS

Don't invoke the god of war, you boy of tears!

CORIOLANUS

Ha!

AUFIDIUS

No more.

CORIOLANUS

Incalculable liar, you make my heart swell beyond the bounds of my chest. "Boy"! Oh, slave! Forgive me, lords, this is the first time that I've ever been forced to scold. My grave lords, you must judge this lowlife to be the liar. Even his own version of events—he who has scars from my sword on his body and must carry the mark of my victory to his grave—will confirm that he's the liar.

FIRST LORD

That's enough, both of you. Hear me speak.

CORIOLANUS

Cut me to pieces, Volsces; men and lads,
Stain all your edges on me. "Boy?" False hound!
If you have writ your annals true, 'tis there,
That, like an eagle in a dove-cote, I
135   Flutter'd your Volscians in Corioles:
Alone I did it. "Boy!"

AUFIDIUS

                Why, noble lords,
Will you be put in mind of his blind fortune,
Which was your shame, by this unholy braggart,
140   'Fore your own eyes and ears?

ALL CONSPIRATORS

                     Let him die for 't.

ALL THE PEOPLE

Tear him to pieces. Do it presently. He kill'd
my son. My daughter. He killed my cousin
Marcus. He killed my father.

SECOND LORD

145   Peace, ho! no outrage: peace!
The man is noble and his fame folds in
This orb o' the earth. His last offences to us
Shall have judicious hearing. Stand, Aufidius,
And trouble not the peace.

CORIOLANUS

150   *(Drawing his sword)*   O that I had him,
With six Aufidiuses, or more, his tribe,
To use my lawful sword!

AUFIDIUS

                 Insolent villain!

ALL CONSPIRATORS

Kill, kill, kill, kill, kill him!

       The Conspirators draw, and kill CORIOLANUS.
            AUFIDIUS *stands on his body.*

LORDS

155   Hold, hold, hold, hold!

CORIOLANUS

Cut me to pieces, Volsces. Men and lads, stain your swords with my blood. "Boy"! Miserable liar! If you've written your histories accurately, it's recorded there that like a wolf in a hen house, I destroyed your Volscians in Corioli. I did it alone. "Boy"!

AUFIDIUS

Noble lords, remember that it was simply good luck that allowed this prideful sinner to cause you this shame, he who now stands before your own eyes and ears.

ALL CONSPIRATORS

Let him die for it.

ALL THE PEOPLE

Tear him to pieces! Do it now! He killed my son! My daughter! He killed my cousin Marcus! He killed my father!

SECOND LORD

Peace! Stop! No outrage. Peace! The man is noble and his fame is known around the world. We will review his most recent offenses fairly in the court of law. Stop, Aufidius, don't disturb the peace.

CORIOLANUS

(Drawing his sword) Oh, I wish I could lawfully kill him and his whole family with my sword.

AUFIDIUS

Contemptuous villain!

ALL CONSPIRATORS

Kill, kill, kill, kill, kill him!

> *The Conspirators draw their swords and kill*
> **CORIOLANUS**. **AUFIDIUS** *stands on his body.*

LORDS

Wait, wait, wait, wait!

AUFIDIUS

My noble masters, hear me speak.

FIRST LORD

O Tullus—

SECOND LORD

Thou hast done a deed whereat valour will weep.

THIRD LORD

Tread not upon him. Masters, all be quiet;
160   Put up your swords.

AUFIDIUS

My lords, when you shall know—as in this rage,
Provoked by him, you cannot—the great danger
Which this man's life did owe you, you'll rejoice
That he is thus cut off. Please it your honours
165   To call me to your senate, I'll deliver
Myself your loyal servant, or endure
Your heaviest censure.

FIRST LORD

Bear from hence his body;
And mourn you for him: let him be regarded
170   As the most noble corse that ever herald
Did follow to his urn.

SECOND LORD

His own impatience
Takes from Aufidius a great part of blame.
Let's make the best of it.

AUFIDIUS

175   My rage is gone;
And I am struck with sorrow. Take him up.
Help, three o' the chiefest soldiers; I'll be one.
Beat thou the drum, that it speak mournfully:
Trail your steel pikes. Though in this city he
180   Hath widow'd and unchilded many a one,
Which to this hour bewail the injury,
Yet he shall have a noble memory. Assist.

Exeunt, bearing the body of CORIOLANUS. *A dead march sounded.*

AUFIDIUS

> My noble masters, hear me speak.

FIRST LORD

> Oh, Tullus—

SECOND LORD

> You've done a dishonorable deed.

THIRD LORD

> Don't stand on him. Noble ones, be quiet. Put away your swords.

AUFIDIUS

> My lords, when you understand—because in this rage he provoked, you cannot—the great danger this man intended to put you in, you'll rejoice that he has been stopped. If your honors will please call me to your Senate, I'll prove myself to have been your loyal servant or endure your strictest punishment.

FIRST LORD

> Step away from his body and mourn for him. Let him be considered as the most noble corpse that a procession has ever followed to a grave.

SECOND LORD

> His own fury frees Aufidius from most of the blame. Let's make the best of it.

AUFIDIUS

> My rage is gone, and I'm full of sorrow. Lift him up. Help, three of the best soldiers. I'll be the fourth. Play the drum in a mournful beat. Lay down your steel spears. Even though he has killed the husbands and children of many people in this city and they're still mourning their loss, we'll give him a noble memorial. Help me.

> *All exit, carrying the body of* CORIOLANUS. *A death march sounds.*

Notes

Notes

Notes

Notes